WHERE'S HARRY?

WHERE'S HARRY?

Steve Stone Remembers His Years with Harry Caray

◆❖◆

STEVE STONE
with Barry Rozner

TAYLOR PUBLISHING
Dallas, Texas

Published by Taylor Publishing Company
1550 West Mockingbird Lane
Dallas, Texas 75235
www.taylorpub.com

Library of Congress Cataloging-in-Publication Data:

Stone, Steve.
    Where's Harry? : Steve Stone remembers his years with
Harry Caray / Steve Stone with Barry Rozner.
        p.   cm.
    ISBN 0-87833-233-2 (alk. paper)
        1. Caray, Harry. 2. Sportscasters—United States—Biography.
3. Chicago Cubs (Baseball team)—History. I. Rozner, Barry.
II. Title.
GV742.42.C37S86   1999
070.4'49796'092—dc21
    [B]   99–11954
                                                        CIP

10 9 8 7 6 5 4 3
Printed in the United States of America

To all the fans who love baseball and have kept a special place in their hearts for Harry Caray.
S.S.

To Amy, my wonderful wife.
To Madisyn and Stefanie, the light of my life.
B.R.

Contents

Foreword by Bob Costas ◇ *ix*

Preface ◇ *xiii*

Introduction ◇ *xv*

Chapter 1   "Where's Harry?" ◇ 1

Chapter 2   "Steve, Where You At?" ◇ 5

Chapter 3   The Gospel According to Harry ◇ 15

Chapter 4   Harry and Tonto ◇ 25

Chapter 5   Indestructible Harry ◇ 35

Chapter 6   "There's Danger Here, Chéri!" ◇ 41

Chapter 7   "The Peplinskis Are Here From. . ." ◇ 51

Chapter 8   "Steve, Where's He Looking?" ◇ 61

Chapter 9   Sanderson to Sundberg to Sandberg ◇ 71

Chapter 10   See No Evil, Hear No Evil, Speak No Evil . . . ◇ 103

Chapter 11   Buy Me Some Ham and Some Cracker Jacks ◇ 109

Chapter 12   Limos, Boats, and All Those Meals ◇ 115

Chapter 13   The Harry Chronicles ◇ 129

Chapter 14   Of Mice and Milo ◇ 143

Chapter 15   Wild About Harry ◇ 151

Chapter 16   The Man, the Mirth, the Legend ◇ 165

Chapter 17   To Your Health ◇ 171

Chapter 18   A Perfect Day ◇ 177

Chapter 19   Take Me Out To the Funeral ◇ 185

Chapter 20   The 10th Inning ◇ 191

Epilogue ◇ 199

Foreword

by Bob Costas

D ecades from now, no matter who is calling baseball in Chicago, through whatever technology, they'll all be compared to Harry Caray. As a symbol of the Cubs (and as a baseball spirit that endures despite the general decline of the game) only Ernie Banks, Ryne Sandberg, and Wrigley Field itself could compare with him. In recent years, among all Chicago sports personalities, only the two Mikes, Jordan and Ditka, were bigger than the man behind the mike.

For years, it seemed, Harry Caray was the Chicago Cubs. And yet, Chicago cannot claim the essential Harry Caray. In truth, his best work came in St. Louis as the voice of the Cardinals.

Back in the '50s and '60s, when baseball was the unquestioned national pastime and when radio, where baseball plays best, was still the primary outlet, Harry was at the peak of his powers. His outsized personality, his authentic passion for the game, and the distinctiveness of his style all combined with extraordinary broadcasting skills. What came out of radios all over St. Louis and the Midwest was so compelling that many clear-thinking people still contend that a Caray broadcast could be more vivid and exciting than attending the game.

I guess I should come clean here. I live in St. Louis. But hold on: I never set foot there until the mid-'70s, after Harry was gone. I didn't grow up a Cardinals fan. Still, my introduction to Harry Caray came in childhood.

As a kid living on New York's Long Island, the Yankees and Mets weren't enough to satisfy my appetite for baseball. This was the Stone Age, pre-ESPN, pre-superstations. The only way to get more baseball was to grab the keys to my father's car and head for the driveway, where radio reception was best. There, at age ten or eleven, I remember turning the car's radio dial like a safecracker, calibrating the millimeters that separated one baseball voice from another. Through the crackle and static they were all there: Bob Prince from Pittsburgh, Ernie Harwell in Detroit, Chuck Thompson out of Baltimore. And on a clear night, from a thousand miles away, here came Harry Caray over KMOX. Not smooth and melodic like Red Barber, Mel Allen, or Vin Scully, but loud and bombastic. So full of energy and heart that even a young Yankees rooter began to believe Sportsman's Park might be the best baseball place on earth. That Stan Musial might be just as heroic as Mickey Mantle.

Years later our paths crossed. Long before I had established much in the way of professional credentials, Harry was very friendly and generous toward me, inviting me into the booth, taking me to dinner. I tried not to show it, but I could never quite get over the fact that I was now friends with the guy who years before had been that unmistakable voice in the night.

Then, as before, no one else had a style quite like Harry's. And it was a style—not a shtick, like so much of what you hear today from broadcasters who think "attitude" can come off an assembly line. Or that a contrived catch phrase here and a "hey look at me" there makes for anything like the authentic personalities of great ones like Harry.

Once, apropos of nothing, it seemed, Harry told me stories of how entertainers befriended him. He counted many, Sinatra and Elvis included, as friends. And why not? Caray himself was a kind of performance artist, working from a broadcast booth instead of a stage.

The Harry Caray to whom Elvis listened has been a memory for quite a while. With age and illness, the skills had diminished, leaving only Harry himself. But he still had the voice, the windshield-size glasses, the love of the game that made him the fans' announcer. And that was good enough.

Some guys can just hold an audience. Elvis knew it. Sinatra knew it. In baseball, no matter the score, fans have never left the park until Ruth, Mays, Sosa, or McGwire has had his last turn at bat. And even if the Cubs trailed by 10, no one ever left Wrigley Field before Harry Caray sang "Take Me Out to the Ball Game." Only then was the experience complete. Only then was the show over. Hey, Elvis, wherever you are, your pal Harry has left the building.

There was, of course, sadness over Harry's passing, and he will long be missed. But what a life he led. And who wouldn't take this deal? You live into your early eighties, you do what you love doing right up until the end, and in the end this can be truthfully said: You made millions of people happy, and millions of people will never forget you. No might be or could be about it. He was . . . Harry Caray. The one and only.

Preface

At least once a day someone asks me about my favorite memory of Harry Caray. And until Feb. 14, 1998, I'm sure that memory would have been of something related to one of our many nights out together.

But it was on that Valentine's Day—the day he left this planet—that I called Harry in Palm Springs to talk about a number of things. Most of them were unimportant, but one thing he said will stay with me forever.

We made small talk for a while and I tried to get him to admit that he was about to turn eighty-four years old on March 1, instead of the seventy-seven he was claiming to be. And after we kidded each other for a while, I got down to the real reason for the call.

I had spent nearly a decade traveling with the Cubs and covering the team for my newspaper, the suburban Chicago *Daily Herald*. But because I had two young children at home, I was getting off the baseball beat and had become a sports columnist. I was thrilled because it was the best thing possible for my family, but it meant I wouldn't be seeing Harry every day anymore.

We had grown close over the years and I was avoiding this conversation, because I wasn't sure how he would react. I had spoken to him several times since I took the new job, but it wasn't until mid-February that I had the nerve to tell Harry the news.

When I told him what I was doing and that I wouldn't see him until late in spring training, Harry stunned me with his reaction.

"Kid, you're doing the right thing for you and your family," Harry said without hesitation, catching me off guard. "You have a bright future with that wife and those kids and I'm glad for you. If I had it to do over again, I wouldn't have missed my kids' growing up. I missed a lot in my life and I have regrets about that. I've always said I don't have many regrets, and that might be the only one, but it's a big one.

"I think I've made up for that in the last few years and now I have a wonderful family. I've become a much happier person because I have a family to share my life with."

And from that moment on, I had a new favorite story about Harry Caray. We made plans for going out to dinner when I arrived in Arizona, and talked about how we looked forward to another year of baseball in 1998. Harry thought the Cubs had a chance to be a much better team, but he still worried about their pitching.

I thanked him for everything he had done for me and for being there whenever I needed advice. He thanked me for buying him a drink a time or two.

We said our good-byes, and that was that. Later that night, he collapsed at a restaurant and never regained consciousness.

Why I called Harry Caray in Palm Springs that Saturday afternoon instead of sometime the next week or the week after that, I'll never know.

But I'll be eternally grateful that I did.

—Barry Rozner

Introduction

spent four and a half years in college. I was married for two and a half years. And I spent fourteen years in professional baseball with many different teams and hundreds of different teammates.

I point this out because for fifteen years Harry Caray and I were partners, and for ten years before that I knew Harry when I was a player and he was a broadcaster. It's without a doubt the longest-lasting relationship of my life.

At various times it took on different looks and variations and encountered different dynamics. It started out as mentor-student. We soon became contemporaries, with Harry acting as an advisor. At times we would become antagonistic and cantankerous, but we grew to be close friends.

We always maintained a mutual respect for the other's abilities. Even during our stormy times, I always knew that I could count on Harry and he could count on me.

The reason I decided to write this book was to give you some insight into a complex man who few people were privileged to know well. Harry was a larger-than-life character who did everything in grand style, from his life to his death.

He truly loved life and embraced every waking moment of it with a vitality that defied the aging process. He did it on his own terms and squeezed every drop of enjoyment out of every day he was given on earth.

But Harry was no saint, and I'm not here to paint you that picture. He certainly wouldn't approve of that. And he had his detractors, but if a measure of a man's life is how many lives he touches, then Harry measures up with anyone I've ever known, heard of, or read about. He certainly had a profound effect on my life, and I wouldn't be where I am today if it hadn't been for Harry Caray.

So if you're looking for the dirt, you won't find it here. I don't have the wisdom to judge Harry. A few people will be more than happy to tell you what Harry wasn't because some people live to diminish the accomplishments of others. I won't waste my time on such pettiness.

But I will tell you what Harry was, and you'll get my honest and humorous look at one of the great legends in broadcasting and baseball history.

The Harry I knew could be mercurial in his moods, critical and caustic, argumentative and combative. The next moment, he could be funny and engaging, insightful and delightful, charming and witty. He also was generous beyond imagination, and he was a dear, dear friend.

When all was said and done, I was Harry's last partner, and for those fifteen years Harry saw to it that I sat in the chair next to him. Like any two partners, we didn't always get along, but deep down there was a very strong bond. On the same day Harry and I went at it on the air pretty good, he came to my fiftieth birthday party, where he kissed me and hugged me and told me that he loved me.

Harry was nothing if not unpredictable.

But after you finish reading this book, I know you'll have a much better understanding of why he did some of the things he did and why he said some of the things he said.

More importantly, you'll have a clearer picture of not just Harry Caray the broadcaster, whom you already know, but Harry Caray the man.

I saw him go from a man who could drink until dawn to a man who could never have another Budweiser. I saw him go from having almost no family to become a loving grandfather of fifteen. I saw him go from a man who did not need anyone to a man who was afraid of dying alone in his hotel room.

I rode on a twenty-five-year emotional roller coaster with Harry and every time I thought I had him figured out, he shocked me with a new twist. Life with Harry was certainly never dull.

I can't completely explain this incredible caricature of a legendary character. Not even Harry could do that. But I think after *Where's Harry?* you'll more fully appreciate a unique and special personality who cared more about you, the fans, than his own survival.

In the end, I hope you'll laugh a little and learn a lot about my friend, Harry Caray.

—Steve Stone

"Where's Harry?"

Harry Caray gazed out at the green grass, the breathtaking ivy and the picturesque shrine known as Wrigley Field and sounded like a man ready to shed a tear.

"What a sensational day for baseball," Harry said softly as he began his soliloquy on a fine summer day in 1989. "Steve, I just can't get over how wonderful the ballpark looks.

"The bleachers are packed and the stands are full and the Cubs are winning and families are here together and . . .

"Hey, wait a minute!" Harry screamed, shattering the peace and calm of the moment. "That's Scottie McKenzie over there on the roof of Murphy's Bleacher bar!"

"Uh, Harry," I said. "If you're talking about the inflatable Budweiser dog, I believe the name you're thinking of is 'Spuds.' He's the Bud Light dog, right?"

"Oh yeah," Harry replied. "Spuds McFadden."

"Uh, no. I don't think so, Harry," I said. "I think it's Spuds McKenzie."

"Yeah, yeah, Steve," Harry said. "Steve McFadden. That's what I said."

"Harry, you're the Bud Man," I said. "You know the name is Spuds McKenzie."

"Yeah, that's right, Steve," Harry agreed. "Murphy McKenzie. The dog's name is Murphy McKenzie. What a beautiful sight on a beautiful day at the ballpark."

"Right, Harry," I said, giving in once and for all. "Murphy McKenzie."

While I spent a good portion of the best years of my adult life having conversations like that with Harry Caray, I spent the rest of it answering questions about him.

In fact, on the very first day I began broadcasting Cubs games for WGN-TV, I heard a question that I would eventually hear about a million times from the hundreds of fans who approached me every day. It was simply this:

"Where's Harry?"

After a few years and several hundred thousand questions, I thought about wearing a T-shirt under my suit that I could pop open every time I was asked, and the shirt would say simply, "How the hell do I know?"

The reality is that no one ever really knew where Harry was, but I think the reason people always asked me was that from the time we started working together to the time Harry left this earth—a span of fifteen years—there was a special bond between us.

The fans viewed us as a team. They didn't see us as two individuals calling baseball in a booth. We were Harry and Steve, together as one. They probably figured we lived together at home and on the road.

It was never, "Hi, Steve, how are you?" or "How are the Cubs going to finish this year?" or "Are you ever going to get married again?"

Nope.

"Where's Harry?"

And though no one really knows the answer to where Harry Caray is now, I have a feeling he's got a Bud in one hand and he's sitting in a seat that everyone can afford. He's entrenched next to a couple of blue-collar baseball fans, and he's still wondering why the Cubs' outfielders can't hit the cutoff man. I really believe that's where Harry is today.

"Where's Harry?" was asked many, many times over the years, but the first time it occurred to me that it meant something special was after a contest in Philadelphia, where the beloved Cubs suffered through yet another excruciating loss, on yet another very warm August evening.

Harry was riding the team bus with us to New York, and that night I received the single indelible image I'll always have of Harry.

For some reason, Harry didn't have a limousine that night and needed a way to get to New York as fast as humanly possible, and the bus was the best way. So we pulled out of Veterans Stadium around 12:30 A.M. and drove the two hours, twenty minutes into Manhattan. As we neared the hotel, it had to be close to 3 A.M.

The players—most of them terrific athletes still in their twenties—were all sleeping, and most of the coaches and broadcasting crew were in some form of semi-coma . . . except for Harry. He'd been awake the entire time and couldn't wait to see the bright lights of the big city.

Finally, after we crossed the last bridge into the Big Apple, Harry leaned over to me and said, "Steve, would you mind taking my bag to the hotel? Thanks, buddy. I really appreciate it. I can't take it where I'm going."

"No problem, Harry," I said. "But, uh, aren't you staying at our hotel?"

"Yeah," he said. "But I got some things to do, and I don't want to carry my bag with me."

And with that, he sauntered up to the front of the bus. We were heading for the Grand Hyatt at 42nd Street and Lexington Avenue, but Harry caught the bus driver—who was barely awake—and said, "Would you mind dropping me off at the next corner?"

We were at about 47th and Lex, which, by the way, is not to be likened to Amsterdam on a Friday evening. This was New York on a Thursday night and not even Rambo ventured out alone in some of these neighborhoods.

"Uh, Mr. Caray," the bussy began, "wouldn't you rather I bring you to the hotel? This isn't a very safe. . . ."

"Listen, pal," Harry interrupted, "I've been married three times. There's nothing out there that scares me."

As Harry let out a whale of laughter, the bus driver stopped in the middle of the intersection. He opened the door for the world's most famous announcer, and Harry shuffled down the steps.

So with very little regard for his personal safety, or much of anything else for that matter, Harry happily disappeared down a darkened and deserted street in search of a couple of cocktails and some conversation about baseball.

That was how Harry lived his life from March 1, 1914, to February 18, 1998. In his nearly eighty-four years on this planet, Harry Caray squeezed more life out of one body than anyone in the history of human bodies. He didn't get cheated out of a swing. He didn't go down looking at a called strike three. He didn't leave anything in the clubhouse.

And as the bus pulled up to the Grand Hyatt at 3 A.M., there were the usual autograph seekers, insomniacs and Harry Caray fans, all of whom shouted that familiar refrain: "Where's Harry?"

And as always, I replied, "Ladies and gentlemen, I don't know. Only Harry knows for sure."

"Steve, Where You At?"

My association with Harry actually began in 1973 during my first stint as a pitcher for the Chicago White Sox. Harry was calling games on TV and radio for the South Side ball club, and we spent a significant amount of time together that season.

But after the season, I was traded across town to the Cubs, where I spent the next three years. Still, I would run into Harry from time to time at various watering holes throughout the Chicago area. But it wasn't until 1977, when I signed with the White Sox as a free agent, that we began to develop a unique relationship that players and broadcasters rarely experience.

Here's how it all started:

Harry lived for many years at the Ambassador East Hotel on the Near North Side of Chicago, and because he stayed at the hotel, the Pump Room just downstairs was one of his favorite watering holes.

At the time, I didn't know about his proclivity for starting at the Pump Room and going on from there until sunrise. But one day early in the '77 season, I stumbled upon Harry at the hotel bar.

Myself and Ken Brett, older brother of the great George Brett and a fellow White Sox pitcher, just happened to be sitting at the bar on an off day enjoying a cocktail or three at about 6 P.M.

"Hey, boys!" Harry yelled to us so that everyone in the place could hear. "How you guys doing? Can I join you?"

"Absolutely," Brett and I said in tandem.

Harry sat with us for a while and we exchanged pleasantries until the Great One just couldn't wait any longer.

Harry was never one to keep much inside and if he had something on his mind, he'd let you know. He was sipping on his drink—and though Harry would probably tell you I never paid for any, I did pay for that one—when he sat back for a minute.

All of a sudden he leaned forward on the bar and got that gleam in his eye. After looking at me, he turned to Brett and said, "What the hell happened to you? Last year, you were a pretty darn good pitcher and this year you're just pitching like crap. What the hell happened? I'll tell you what, you better start pitching better or find another line of work, young man."

Needless to say, both Ken and I were taken aback. Obviously more Ken than I since it was Brett he was ripping to shreds.

"I don't know, Harry," Brett replied after catching his breath. "But if I knew the reason, I probably wouldn't be nearly as bad as I've been this year."

We eventually changed the subject and had some great laughs with Harry as he dragged us all over town, from spot to spot, from club to club, and from bar to bar. He was, after all, "the Mayor of Rush Street."

But I knew from that day on that if Harry had something to say, he wouldn't beat around the bush. He'd let you know exactly what was on his mind, and he went on to prove that over and over again in the twenty-five years we knew each other.

And that was something I always admired about him, because there was no b.s. with Harry. What you saw on TV was exactly the way he was in real life. He didn't turn it on and off for the cameras. That was just Harry being Harry.

"Hey, there's Connie Stevens," he yelled as the beautiful entertainer strolled into our booth one day in 1986. "My God! How old are you? You've been around forever. You must really be getting up there."

And if you bumped into him on the street he would've been the same person, and I'm convinced that's the reason he was so beloved. He was honest and true to the fans. They were the ones he felt he was working for, not the owners. Don't get me wrong, because he sold the game better than anyone I've ever known, but he really didn't sugarcoat anything just to get people in the park.

Near the conclusion of a special in 1987, Harry and I discussed night baseball and the looming prospect of lights at Wrigley Field. Harry blasted the idea and made it clear he was entirely opposed to the idea.

After we were finished taping, Harry yelled, "Now, you guys keep that piece in about how I hate night baseball. I'm not afraid of what management will say. The fans are the ones who pay my salary, so you keep that part in there about night baseball."

Over his last few years, the Cubs were so bad that at times he probably did a better selling job than at other times. Maybe he held back a little bit, but on the other hand, anyone sitting at home could have seen how bad the Cubs were. Harry didn't have to beat that horse to death.

Over the years, though, he made a career out of telling the truth. How many other broadcasters would have had the courage and the self-confidence to get away with that?

After that initial encounter with Harry at the bar, he and I had many discussions about baseball and pitching, and he often took me to task for something that happened on the mound while I was with the White Sox. Harry would frequently question me about a mistake I made or a screw-up that he believed was my fault.

But I never made an excuse. I think Harry respected the fact that I didn't make excuses. If I made a bad pitch or a bad decision, that's all there was to it. I knew early on that Harry was the kind of guy who didn't mind telling it like it was, and he certainly didn't want to hear anything else.

I believe it was that initial honesty we had in our conversations that eventually led Harry to champion my involvement with WGN.

When I retired from baseball in June 1982 because of an arm injury, I immediately went to work for ABC doing Monday Night Baseball. Among my partners were the likes of Howard Cosell, Al Michaels, Keith Jackson, Bob Uecker, and Don Drysdale.

And even though I'd spent my last four years pitching in Baltimore, I'd always thought of Chicago as a place I'd like to make my home. I'd grown up in Cleveland, and Chicago was very similar in many ways, only much bigger.

After living in Chicago for six years while playing with both the Cubs and White Sox, I'd kept much of my personal life alive in the Windy City, despite the distance. I still had my dentist and my barber in Chicago and visited them when I could make it to town.

So on one August day in 1982, I was headed to Milwaukee to broadcast a game for ABC, and I decided to stop in Chicago along the way. I figured I could stay at the Ambassador East, drop in on some old friends, and enjoy what Chicago had to offer for a couple of days.

At the time, I didn't know Harry was still living at the Ambassador East during the summers, or that he had become the play-by-play man for the Cubs prior to the '82 season, when he and the White Sox parted company.

On my final morning in the city, I left my room and went down to the newspaper stand with plans to drive on up to

Milwaukee that night. But as I went down to get a paper, I heard a bellhop tell the woman at the desk that he had some newspapers for Mr. Caray.

I stopped the young man, took one of my cards out, and put my room number on it. I asked the kid to please give it to Harry and I went back to my room.

Sure enough, two minutes later, the phone rang.

"Steve?" Harry said. "Where you at?"

"Harry," I said laughing, "I'm in the hotel. Where do you think I am? You just called me, remember?"

"Oh yeah," Harry said. "What's going on, buddy? What are you doing in town?"

I explained that I was on my way to Milwaukee to do an ABC game and that I was going to see the dentist.

"Well," Harry said. "You know what? They're looking for a partner for me for the WGN games and I gave them three names I'd be interested in and your name was one of them. Don't leave your room. I have to make a call, and I'll have them call you."

Within five minutes, Jim Dowdle, the head of Tribune Company broadcasting at the time, phoned me and said, "Would you be interested in coming down to talk about this?"

"Sure," I said. "I'll be happy to talk about it."

I didn't know what to think because I really didn't have the financial need to take a job right away. I was getting paid by ABC, and I had deferred half of my salary every year in Baltimore so that for at least four years after I retired I wouldn't be forced into taking a job I didn't want.

But I went down to Tribune Tower to see Jim Dowdle, and we had a great conversation. It was mostly philosophy about baseball and a little about broadcasting, but nothing really specific about the job itself.

I asked if they were going to hire a full-time color guy to sit next to Harry and he said he wasn't sure what they'd do. They were exploring all the options, but if they did hire a color man, he would consider me as one of the viable candidates. He did warn me, however.

"If this is just a passing fancy for you," Dowdle said, "then don't take the WGN job. But if you want this for a career, 150 games a year as a color guy working with Harry Caray in Chicago, this is probably the best situation you could be involved in."

Well, having lived in Chicago and having played for both teams on both sides of town, I knew Chicago was a great city, but I had no idea at the time how good of a job it would be to work as Harry's sidekick at WGN.

About six weeks went by without so much as a word from Harry Caray or Jim Dowdle or anyone from WGN, so I didn't think much more about it. And then one day, out of the blue, I got a call from Dowdle.

"Steve," Dowdle said. "I think you ought to fly to Chicago."

"Why?" I asked.

"Just fly in," Dowdle said, "and we'll talk about it."

So I flew into O'Hare Airport, took a cab downtown, met with Jim Dowdle, and was immediately told I had the job. At no time during any conversation did he mention money or contract length or any terms at all. I had no idea about any of it. I just knew I was Harry Caray's partner, and I had the feeling that Harry would have a monumental say in how long I'd be his partner. It was, after all, Harry who was responsible for me getting the job in the first place.

And that's something I'll never forget as long as I live.

Having been married once when I was young, I can tell you my relationship with Harry was like a marriage in many ways. We had our great times and tough times. Our fun discussions and our arguments. Our ups and our downs. But never did we stop caring about each other, and never did either of us say we couldn't live together anymore.

Looking back on it now, I realize I probably spent more time with Harry than I did with anyone else my entire life.

Put that in your cigar and smoke it.

As close as we were during the baseball season, Harry and I rarely spoke during the winters, except during the times when something major was occurring. For example, after the 1987 season, when Harry knew I was interested in pursuing a front office job with the Cubs, we spoke a few times a week.

Dallas Green had been fired, and at that time I decided I'd like to try to get the job as general manager of the Cubs. That's the first time I went to Tribune Company executive John Madigan asking him if he'd consider me for that position.

Harry knew of my desires and was very encouraging because, I think, he had a lot of confidence in my abilities as a baseball man, not just a broadcaster. I know he made some calls on my behalf, so we spoke quite often during the winter following the 1987 season.

The only other time we conversed a lot during an off-season was one year before that—after Harry had suffered his stroke in the spring of 1987. Uncharacteristically, Harry called me three times that spring and never seemed to have anything in particular he wanted to discuss. The third time he called, I just had a feeling he was on the phone for a specific reason. Being an orphan and probably the most independent man I've ever known, Harry was never one to say, "I need help," or "I need you," but that's what I felt he wanted to say.

He was trying to tell me that he was nervous about returning after the stroke and that he might need some help getting through those first couple of weeks of the baseball season.

"Harry, there's nothing to worry about," I said. "You were there for me at the beginning and you're the big reason I'm here now. You taught me how to broadcast and you taught me how to be accepted in this market."

Without question, Harry was responsible for my being in that booth. If at any time during our fifteen years he didn't want me there anymore, I wouldn't have been there. I would've been out looking for another job. I owed him a lot, and there was really nothing I could ever do to repay him. If letting him lean on me a bit was something he wanted, I would certainly do that.

And though Harry wasn't frequently given to emotional moments and warm thank-yous, he did appreciate me. We had a mutual respect and admiration, and Harry made us into a good team.

"When you do come back," I told Harry on that spring day in '87, "I know you'll need some help, and as long as you need me in the booth, I'll be there for you."

Harry didn't say a word about it. He just said, "I'll see you in May." It was May 19, 1987, to be exact, and that led to one of my greatest memories of Harry Caray.

Harry had suffered a debilitating stroke and missed the first seven weeks of the baseball season. For a short time he'd lost the ability to speak and some movement in certain areas of his body.

Slowly but surely, it all came back to him, and by May 19, Harry was ready to call his first game of the season.

You think he needed help? You think he eased back into it? You think he was nervous? Not a chance. Not Harry.

He came right back and in characteristic style, called nine innings of play-by-play like he'd never missed a day.

Once the day was over, he told me the only time he'd been nervous the entire day was prior to the seventh-inning stretch, when everyone at Wrigley Field stood in unison and chanted his name before the Cubs had even retired the side in the top of the inning.

"I had tears in my eyes, Steve," Harry said. "I was just hoping I didn't screw it up."

He didn't, but that's not what I remember most about that magical day. The most amazing thing occurred when Harry got a phone call in the booth early in the game. It was from the

President of the United States, Ronald Reagan, himself a Cub fan and once a broadcaster, too.

The team and the station had gone to incredible lengths to get the call arranged and it happened right on schedule. As the bottom of the first inning was about to begin, the call was beamed through to the WGN-TV listeners and there was President Reagan telling Harry how wonderful it was to have him back. The president talked about how the entire country was excited and happy to have Harry in the broadcast booth once again.

He went on and on with glowing praise reserved more for ex-presidents and heads of state than a baseball play-by-play man, but that's the effect Harry had on people—even the president.

Mr. Reagan continued on for about two or three minutes and as the president was mentioning Nancy Reagan and her strong ties to Chicago, and the couple's history with the city, Harry suddenly interrupted him. The only one more stunned than me was President Reagan.

"Excuse me, Mr. President," Harry said, "but Bobby Dernier just got a bunt single and I gotta get back to the baseball game."

Click!

He hung up on the President of the United States.

Harry was probably the only man in the country who felt a Bobby Dernier bunt single was more important than talking to the most powerful man in the world. But that story typifies how Harry viewed life. There was nothing more important to him than the game of baseball, and when it was time to call baseball, Harry called baseball—president or no president.

And when the inning came to an end, Harry turned to me sitting beside him and said, "Steve, where were you while I was on the phone with the president?"

"Right here, Harry," I said with a chuckle. "Right where I always am. Right here next to you."

The Gospel According to Harry

When we first started teaming up, Harry was generous with both his praise and his criticism of my broadcasting style because he knew exactly what needed to be said to relate to the fans at home.

He also knew that my first broadcasting experience was with a national network and that local broadcasting was considerably different from the network version.

So Harry actually shaped the type of color man he wanted me to become, even though he hadn't worked much on network TV.

For instance, the first thing Harry taught me was that I was there in the booth for the fans, and not for anyone else. There's a line he used many times over the years and it went something like this:

"There've been a lot of times during my career when ball players really disliked me and many times when ownership really disliked me and so many times when a manager and general manager didn't like me. But one of the reasons I've kept my job all these years is that the fans have always loved me."

Essentially, that's for whom Harry taught me to broadcast. I think Harry felt like he was the voice of the fans and that he was the voice of the common man.

Harry also knew of my educational background, and though I was never a Rhodes Scholar, one thing I had a tendency to do was talk above my audience. That's something Harry set out to try to improve right off the bat.

After our first year together in 1983, Harry told me he thought I was going to be a great broadcaster, but he wanted to think of a way to humanize me more for the fans.

"I'm going to think about it over the winter," Harry said. "And next year, Steve, we're going to have a new routine."

When we got to spring training in 1984, he said he had an idea.

"You know, Steve," Harry said with his customary start to a conversation, "the network broadcasts are stiffer than our broadcasts. We have a homier feel and people feel like they're our friends and that we come into their homes and share the game with them. We need to do more of that."

Now I'm not saying that Harry didn't make mistakes, because he made a million of them, but just as many things you thought were mistakes were no accident at all.

Harry had a great sense of what it took to sell the game to the fans. One of his favorite things to do was to hold up a glass of what appeared to be beer, though you might find it interesting to discover that it was really only a glass of water.

He wanted people to believe he was drinking during the game, just like they were at home, and a great fallacy is that he was drunk during so many of those broadcasts. That was just Harry's way of making the fans feel comfortable. He gave them the impression that he was sitting in the bar with them having a drink and discussing the game.

But in my fifteen years with him, Harry might've had a grand total of twenty beers during games. They were always Budweisers and usually in St. Louis since the tap was so close to the broadcast booth at Busch Stadium. Harry might've felt closer to Bud there than in any other city.

In any case, "Harry the Bud Man" was just an image he wanted to promote because he felt his blue-collar following could relate to that Harry, and he had a very strong grasp of what his audience could relate to.

So when we came back to baseball in 1984, Harry brought with him the idea of cigars. Yes, the cigars.

Most people think I was born with a cigar in my mouth, but the truth is I smoked a pipe most of the time and had maybe one cigar a week before Harry introduced the idea.

Harry felt that the pipe was an image for an educated fan, and that's not the image he wanted for me. He believed the baseball fan was someone who pictured the writers and the broadcasters drinking a few beers and smoking a few cigars.

So Harry got me started on the cigars and even bought me the first box, and then every time I would smoke a cigar in the booth he would go on a lengthy tirade.

"How can a smart guy like you with a fine education sit there with a stinking, ugly, filthy, cheap cigar?" he'd yell.

He did it over and over and over again as he tried to show the audience that I was really just an average guy, but after a while I really believed it bothered him.

In fact, I was getting about 200 cigars a week from people who loved the shtick and wanted to see Harry with a bur under his saddle, so they'd send cigars with a note that said something like, "Here, blow this at Harry and see if he likes this better." Those were the really stinky ones.

But I thought I was really offending him, so one night we had a few cocktails and some dinner and I said, "Harry, if the cigar thing really bothers you that much, I could stop."

"Are you kidding me?" Harry said, bursting out laughing. "I've spent my entire life in smoke-filled booths and taverns, and ours is an open-air box. It doesn't bother me. I came up with the idea to humanize you more."

That was a breakthrough for us as a team in 1984. That was Harry's attempt at bringing me closer to the fans, but at the same time he would point out the difference between us on the broadcast.

He would portray me as the educated businessman, intimating that I came from a privileged background, when essentially we came from very similar backgrounds financially.

Harry was an orphan in St. Louis and was very, very poor growing up. I was much more fortunate because I had a family, thank God, but we were not well off. Growing up in Cleveland, my mother was a waitress in a shot-and-a-beer bar, and my father changed records in jukeboxes. I was anything but privileged.

If you ever had a conversation with him away from the booth, then you also know that Harry was a brilliant businessman and was extremely bright when it came to current events, history, politics, and most other matters. Believe me, Harry was no dummy. It was quite to the contrary.

But Harry liked to play up that imaginary difference in our childhoods and in our education and in our business interests. He always played up the fact that he was a man of the people and a guy who could relate to the common baseball fan.

That was never better illustrated than on the night of August 8, 1988, when Wrigley Field turned on the lights and played a night game for the first time in its history. It's my contention to this day that it was Harry's idea that each broadcaster wear a tuxedo that night, since it was such an important occasion.

So as we all got up to our booths before the game, all decked out in fine formal wear, in walked Harry wearing a pair of slacks and a flannel shirt that made him look like Paul Bunyan.

Some might suggest that it was Harry's way of reminding everyone of his perpetual campaign against night baseball at

Wrigley Field. But I think Harry planned it all that way to remind everyone that he was just a regular guy and the rest of us were something else entirely.

That was pure Harry.

Harry was constantly searching for new ways to widen this imaginary educational gap between us, so one day he chose an Arne Harris hat shot to make his point. Arne, the legendary WGN-TV producer/director, was famous for the hat shots that he encouraged his cameramen to find, and on this particular day in 1986, Arne's Army found a guy with a unicorn hat. Why, I don't know, but the fact is the guy had a horn sticking out of his forehead.

"There's another Arne Harris hat shot and this guy's wearing a unicorn hat on his head," I said with great insight.

"What in the world is that?" Harry said. "What's a umicorm?"

"It's not a 'umicorm.' It's a unicorn, Harry, and it's a mythical horse with a horn coming out of its forehead. And that guy has one on his hat."

"Well, c'mon, Steve," Harry whined, pretending to be irritated. "Why don't you just say it's a mythical horse with a horn coming out of its forehead?"

"But I said it was a unicorn, Harry."

"Well," Harry replied, "I don't know why you have to use those big Harvard words all the time."

In those early years with Harry, he went on to show me time and time again that he was a walking, talking, and drinking contradiction.

On the one hand he was trying to get people to relate to

me more, but on the other hand he was promoting the gap between us by trying to make himself look like a man of the people.

It made for good television.

He showed me quickly that by pointing up the difference between us, we could maintain a great routine for a very long time. Harry said that contrast of styles is the way it should be. He said two of him in the booth would be too overbearing and two of me would be too dull, but one of each of us would be a good broadcasting team.

"I'll be the screaming guy," Harry said. "I'll get excited and yell and cheer and be disappointed. Those will be my true emotions and I'll let them spill out onto the air. I won't be acting, Steve, because that's what I feel.

"You, on the other hand, you have to be the cool, analytical voice of reason. You're the ex-player and you have to explain whatever my emotion is. You have to explain why I'm excited or disappointed.

"So I'll scream and you analyze and it'll work out fine that way."

Harry also told me to expect an argument even when there wasn't any reason for one.

"It's OK for us to argue," Harry said. "Even when I agree with you, I might disagree just to keep it interesting. In fact, if we can argue a lot that'll be even better."

Harry Caray had the greatest sense of theater of any broadcaster I've ever come across on any level, and he knew how to get the most out of a situation and deliver the results to the fans. The truth of the matter is that Harry really cared about the fans, and he was concerned about giving them the most entertainment possible. That's something he stressed to me quite often.

Early on in our partnership, Harry reminded me of a time in the mid-'70s when he and Chuck Tanner, the former White Sox manager, got into a feud, which manifested itself on a daily basis either on the field or in the dugout prior to each game.

Tanner was angry about things Harry was saying on the air, and the two men began trading potshots. Tanner would rip Harry in the papers, and Harry would get back at him on his broadcasts.

This went on for a while before Harry confronted Tanner and said, "Chuck, if we're going to hate each other, let's hate each other on the pregame show on radio and on TV. Let's quit doing this for the newspapers. I'm in the TV and radio business.

"Let's get it all on the radio show and do it on TV and we'll sell more advertising and get more listeners and viewers."

So it became even more controversial on the pregame shows. That was Harry. He was never one to let anything get by that would enhance the broadcast. He knew what was best, and that's what was best.

There's no doubt that baseball was Harry's main interest, but he also liked politics and world affairs.

And the thing he liked most in life was arguing.

"Steve," Harry began one day, "I really like to argue."

"Harry," I chuckled, "believe it or not, I've noticed that."

"Just so you know," Harry said, "I'll take the opposite side of an argument just to get a conversation going and play devil's advocate. I've made a career out of that. After all, that's what baseball is all about. There's always more than one way to do something in baseball and it's fun to talk and argue about it. That's good TV.

"Steve, I just say what I feel. I'm a fan who happens to have a microphone, and the fans like that because someone is say-ing it the way they would if they had a mike."

And when it came down to calling an important play, Harry

wasn't about to pull any punches. But the odd thing is, some people called him a homer.

"How could that be, Steve?" he'd wonder. "Just ask Keith Moreland if he thinks I tell the truth. I love my team and I want them to win every game, but when a ball goes through a guy's legs, what am I supposed to do, say he looked good? Or if a guy pops out with the bases loaded in the ninth with the game on the line, I can't say he did a good job."

True professionals have no problem with that because they know before anyone else when they've made a mistake, and if you listen closely, you'll notice the superstars are often the first ones to plead guilty. So most of the players who worked in front Harry over the years liked him a lot and some of them truly loved him. I think all of them at least respected him for saying what he believed.

But Harry was the ultimate fan and the consummate front-runner, which he readily admitted. If a player was having a bad season and wasn't a big star, he was going to incur Harry's wrath from time to time. Harry just couldn't stand a lack of effort or sloppy play. It drove him crazy, so there were players that became targets, like Dick Ruthven and Keith Moreland on the North Side and Rick Reichardt and Bill Melton on the South Side. They didn't care too much for Harry, but that sentiment wasn't echoed by many.

When Harry switched from the South Side White Sox to the North Side Cubs, there was much thought that the conservative Cubs ownership wouldn't take kindly to Harry's style. But he wasn't about to change after almost forty years.

"I've never cared a day in my life what an owner or manager or player or general manager thought about what I said," Harry said. "I don't care if they're mad at me. Baseball fans are baseball fans and they don't care what management says either. I always said what I felt and I wasn't about to stop just because I switched teams.

"When I switched from St. Louis to Oakland, I learned the most important lesson of all. It's not the name of the city across the uniform or the name of the team or the stars on the field. It's the game that matters.

"We're all just temporary actors on a stage. Players come and go, owners come and go, and broadcasters come and go, but the game lives on. People love the game. I could go out and call a Little League game and be just as excited as I am calling this game. I know Bill Veeck felt the same way about the game, and that's why he was able to make it fun for the only people that matter: the fans.

"I wish I could say there's one around like Bill Veeck still, but no one in the game today understands how to provide the fans some enjoyment and make money at the same time. The fans just want to have a good time. But big business makes it impossible for a guy like him to be around today."

And unfortunately for the average fan, Harry isn't around to stick up for you anymore, either.

Harry and Tonto

While Harry and I used to argue on the air, mostly for entertainment purposes, I didn't know how much we'd argue for real later in our association.

You see, by the mid-'80s, I was heavily into the restaurant/bar business with the brilliant restaurateur, Rich Melman, in both Chicago and Phoenix. There came a point when Harry decided he'd like to get involved with me in a business venture, too.

This was before he had Harry Caray's restaurant in Chicago and so we decided to open two spots in Arizona; one in Scottsdale and one in Mesa, the spring training home of the Cubs.

At the time, sports bars were becoming the in-thing so we invited Harry in and decided to open up a couple of sports bars. The first name we came up with was "Steve and Harry's," but it didn't last long.

"Steve," Harry said with a laugh, "if I'm going to be involved in this, it's going to have to go the other way."

So we quickly changed it to "Harry and Steve's" and that was OK with me. Harry always wanted top billing, and I didn't care.

I was sort of like Murray on *The Mary Tyler Moore Show*. Some days Murray had a bigger part than other days, but it was always the *The Mary Tyler Moore Show* and she was still the star of the show.

In my case, it was always the "Harry Caray Show" and I knew that. Eventually, *The Love Boat* came along for Murray, but in Chicago that wasn't to be the case for me. I understood the pecking order, and I had no problem with that. I never forgot that it was Harry who was responsible for my being there in the first place.

Well, the restaurant partnership seemed like such a great idea at the beginning, but in time it became a bone of contention between us. While we struggled a bit with "Harry and Steve's," "Harry Caray's" opened in downtown Chicago a couple of years later with no investment from Harry at all. Just for the use of his name, Harry began raking in some serious dollars. He got a 3.5 percent take, and in 1997 they did $7 million worth of business. That was almost $250,000 for Harry.

So, as you can see, he was pulling in hundreds of thousands of dollars a year in Chicago, but his investment with us in Arizona wasn't going too well.

The reality is that downtown Scottsdale and midtown Mesa are not exactly the same as the Near North Side in Chicago, and if it wasn't spring training, Harry's name just didn't have the same effect. Harry wasn't making the same kind of money in Arizona as he was in Chicago, but what he didn't realize is that I wasn't making any money, either.

The two restaurants in Arizona probably lost a half-million dollars over those years, and Harry never quite understood why he wasn't able to reap the benefit of his name in Mesa like he did in Chicago.

It became something that, for a time, started to strain a good relationship.

As Harry became more frustrated with our business relationship, he began to take our arguments a little more seriously on the air.

When I first joined Harry in 1983, we could argue and

debate vigorously on or off the air and as soon as we were done, everything was fine again. But as he got older, he almost took our difference of opinion personally.

That was never more apparent than on one of the greatest nights in Cubs history: September 26, 1989. That was the night the Cubs clinched the Eastern Division title at Montreal's Olympic Stadium.

I was completely drenched in champagne from the locker room celebration. I had it in my eyes and on my head and down my pants and in my shoes. Needless to say, I was a mess. I looked like a drowned rat. My eyes hurt. If you've ever had four bottles of champagne dumped on your head, you know what I mean. If not, then I don't suggest you experiment with it.

So I couldn't wait to get back to the hotel and clean up and then get out on the town for a big night of partying. But in the limo riding home after the celebration, Harry and I got into it for the most ridiculous reason.

Here we were, going to celebrate with the entire hierarchy of WGN and Tribune Company, and Harry wanted to fight about Doug Dascenzo, the diminutive outfielder for the Cubs. Harry's contention was that Dascenzo could be the starter if he ever got the chance to play every day.

"I'm telling you, Steve," Harry bellowed. "This guy could be a great player if anyone ever let him play."

"I think you're overstating it a little bit, don't you, Harry?" I replied. "I mean he's the size of a jockey, but he could be a nice fourth outfielder if he was used correctly. But he can't bunt and he can't really hit. He's terrific defensively. That makes him a solid fourth outfielder."

And then Harry went ballistic.

"You're just like the rest of them," he screamed at me as everyone else ducked for cover. "You'll never give him a chance because he's a little guy. I don't understand you guys."

"I can't give him a chance, Harry," I said. "I'm not the

manager. I'm your partner. I don't make out the lineup card. Besides, aren't you always saying I always stick up for the little guys?"

But Harry wouldn't let it go. He said Dascenzo would be the next great center fielder. He never did stop talking about Doug Dascenzo his whole career.

There were instances like that when it felt like Harry was taking it all personally and our relationship started to deteriorate.

Probably the most famous example of our on-air disputes took place at Shea Stadium on September 28, 1990, on a cold and rainy New York night.

WGN-TV always had a policy that during rain delays, we would keep the feed live from the stadium, and we were expected to stay in the booth and broadcast throughout the delay. That's always been the WGN philosophy and it's led to some outstanding moments in TV—and some embarrassing moments. Harry and I were involved in many of both.

During this particular rain delay, we began discussing the Cubs and their farm system, a topic Harry and I spent a lot of time discussing whether it was on or off the air. We were mentioning the lack of ability to develop quality pitchers, another subject we spent a lot of time on.

Now, I think people truly believe that what they were hearing on the air was 100 percent honesty. It was close, but not 100 percent, because Harry felt as though there were things that we knew that we didn't have to say to the general public.

But the truth is during the years Jim Frey was the general manager (1987-91), it was a stagnant period for the Cubs as far as the farm system is concerned. Most of the players produced by the Dallas Green years were in Chicago and the system had fallen on hard times. For myriad reasons, there was very little talent down on the farm.

But you can't come on the broadcast and lay out chapter and verse about how bad the farm system is, because you don't want to tell people that there's no hope for the rest of eternity. So, we were breaking down the organization and not telling any lies, but being a tad diplomatic.

Harry was very diplomatic about a newly hired GM until he saw which way the wind was blowing. When he saw a GM in trouble, then Harry was much more willing to discuss a general manager's inadequacies.

On this rainy night, we were debating the merits of the farm system when we finally broke away for a commercial after about forty-nine minutes. (Arne Harris was always generous in that regard. He liked to see us dripping wet before he'd let us wipe our faces and get a sip of water.)

The thing is, from our talks off the air and in the limos after the games, Harry and I both realized the organization was going nowhere and there was trouble in the minors.

And as we came back from the break, Harry asked me what I thought about the young pitchers in the system. I said there were no Greg Maddux types out there, but perhaps with some patience and some teaching, maybe the Cubs will find someone with some talent to get up to the majors over the next couple of years.

That's when Harry decided to embarrass me.

"Steve," he hollered, "why don't you say on the air what you tell me off-camera and between innings?"

He was implying that I was less honest with the fans than he was. Hey, Harry was the same as me and said many of the same things I had said. And although that very much angered me at the time, I was careful with my response.

I said I didn't think there were many pitchers down in the minors but the Cubs weren't the only ones going through it. It was pretty much the same thing all over baseball. Very few teams had enough pitchers and it was a common thread throughout the game.

I didn't fire back at Harry or anything like that. I would

never consider putting on the air the things we said to each other off the air.

Harry was the ultimate front runner if a team was great. Everything was wonderful. But if a team was bad, everything was terrible. That was his true emotion, so you can't fault him for that. Harry mirrored the fan. If things were good, he wouldn't look for the bad, and when things were bad, he had a hard time finding the good.

Although Harry took pride in his image of telling it like it was, he had a product to sell. In selling this product, he didn't want to turn up the spotlight on the areas left undiscovered until they had to be uncovered.

Broadcasters around teams are privy to a lot of information, and they have to use their discretion. There are certain ways to phrase criticism and that's part of understanding what being a broadcaster on the local level is all about.

So why did Harry choose that moment to embarrass me? I think he did it because of something going on in our personal or business lives, and it wasn't good for either of us.

The next morning I was awakened in my hotel room by a phone call from Chicago morning radio personality Jonathon Brandmeier. I realized that if it wasn't a potential powder keg, then at the very least it was bad publicity for both of us.

Johnny wanted to know what the deal was and suggested Harry was mad at me. He implied that there was a huge rift.

"Oh, no," I said. "In fact, I had to stop and think about what you're talking about. Johnny, that was just Harry being Harry. He says what's on his mind and there's really no problem at all."

Essentially, it went away after that, but I realized at that point that things had really deteriorated.

That's when I finally made an accommodation to buy Harry out of the restaurant business, and we dissolved our business relationship. Thereafter, everything went back to the way it was before and Harry and I never had a cross word again.

Like I said, I think our relationship was almost like a marriage. You have your rocky times and your misunderstandings, but we had a wonderful relationship before and after the business thing ended. Most people didn't know about that and thought we were having lots of problems, but really that wasn't the case.

Through it all, Harry always respected my ability as a broadcaster and as a baseball person, and I always respected his ability to stir fans to a fever pitch during a game. He'll always be the most charismatic broadcaster in the history of the business and the most beloved play-by-play man any team could ever have.

That mutual respect never diminished.

The fact is, we were partners once and forever.

Period.

Still, I never knew what to expect from Harry on a day-to-day basis, and I was never sure how he'd react to anything I did or said.

One time a reporter asked me some questions about what would happen if Harry ever stepped down, and did I think I was the heir apparent.

"Of course not," I said. "Absolutely not. My role is that of the color analyst and I'd have no different job if Harry left. It's not my job to get. They would certainly bring in another play-by-play man, so there would be no advantage for me at all. As a partner, I'd be losing the most colorful guy in the game. Harry should broadcast as long as he's physically capable of doing it, because the Cubs don't have much to sell at the moment besides the ivy and Harry."

I thought it was all very flattering and complimentary toward Harry when I read it in the paper the next morning and as I walked into the booth that day, I had already forgotten about the story.

But Harry hadn't. He looked over at me and set his books down on the table. He stared at me for a second and then said, "So you think you can take my job, huh?"

"What?" I asked. "What . . . take your job?"

"You think you can take my job?" Harry repeated.

Then it hit me: he had read the newspaper article. Of course he did. He read the papers every morning. He loved newspapers. But this time he thought he had read something that he didn't. It said nothing like that.

"You think you can take my job?" he asked for the third time. "Go ahead. Try and take my job."

"Harry," I pleaded. "That's not what the story said. I said there's no way in the world I'd take the job because it's not mine to take."

"Well, if you think you're good enough to take my job, then go ahead and try," Harry bellowed. "You really think you can do this job?"

"Harry," I finally said. "I don't want your job. I hope you broadcast another twenty years because whenever you're done broadcasting, they're going to bring in another play-by-play guy. It's not gonna be me."

We had a few of those strange conversations over the years, but eventually we wound up laughing and dropping the whole thing. But you have to understand that Harry was a guy who came from nothing and wasn't about to give up any ground without a fight. From me, of course, he was never going to get one, but he was fiercely protective anyway. Of his position, of his power, of his fame, and of his domain.

And I understood that completely.

Before Harry became one of the great defenders of Pete Rose, that very same player was the cause of one our biggest arguments. Shortly after I got the job, Harry and I got to talking one day, and we somehow got on the subject of Pete Rose and Rod Carew. I took the side of Rose and he took the side of Carew, who was obviously one of the greatest hitters of all time.

"You're just like everyone else," Harry yelled. "You say Carew was a good player but he never hit for power and he never went to a World Series and all of that."

"Harry," I said, "I'm just telling you that Rose missed a total of sixty games in his first twenty years and Rod used to miss sixty a year in some seasons. I just don't see how you can debate the virtue of a player who you know will be there every single day."

Things swung a different way when it came to Rose's betting scandal and his legal problems. And always having the need to be contrary, Harry became the champion of Pete Rose's cause. He read the commissioner's report and was very upset by the findings of baseball against Rose.

"Look who's testifying against Pete Rose," Harry said. "They've got bookmakers and bartenders and guys from the track and a bunch of guys with questionable character."

"Harry," I said, "this case is about gambling and you're going to find some shady characters involved. Do you think they're going to let nuns and priests testify against him? All the guys he was involved with were bookmakers and bartenders and guys from the track."

He thought Pete should be in the Hall of Fame and didn't care what he did wrong. He was looking at his accomplishments and nothing else.

"Why don't they show us the proof if there's so much proof?" Harry asked repeatedly. "There's no proof!"

I'll say one thing about Harry: If he believed in it, he was going to fight for it until there was no fight left in you, and he often left me for dead.

CHAPTER 5

Indestructible Harry

The stroke of 1987 was one of the rare times that Harry Caray showed himself to be even the least bit vulnerable.

I personally saw him survive falls and pratfalls that would've killed many a younger man, and considering Harry was in his late '70s or early '80s when many of these incidents occurred, it's quite amazing that he survived.

What it all comes down to is that Harry was basically indestructible.

The 1994 season was a particularly rough one for Harry and his first fall took place on April 7, the day Michael Jordan appeared for the White Sox in an exhibition game against the Cubs at Wrigley Field.

It was a wonderful experience for all of us, and Harry in particular enjoyed watching the greatest basketball player of all time perform well on the greatest baseball field of all time.

It was a long day followed by a long night and a difficult flight to Montreal, during which a few cocktails—and little food—were ingested.

We landed at about 2 A.M. and in every other city Harry would have immediately jumped into his limo and been off into the night, on his way to his favorite dining establishment. But in Montreal, we all had to go through customs, so there was Harry walking through the Canadian airport with all the rest of us.

As we got near the customs agents, there was a huge wet spot on the floor and a maintenance man was mopping up a hallway. There was no sign saying, "Caution: Wet Floor." There was no warning in English or French or any language for that matter.

We were all telling Harry to be careful when he turned to us and said, "Don't worry, boys. If I slip, I'll sue these airport sons-of- . . ." But before he could even finish his sentence, both feet went straight out from under him and his briefcase and glasses went flying high into the air.

There was nothing to break his fall except the cement, which nearly broke his back. Harry hit the back of his head and neck and didn't move a muscle for what seemed like an eternity.

I held my breath as we raced over to pick him up. When we did, the eighty-year-old immortal bounced up, straightened his coat, put his glasses back on, and picked up his briefcase.

"Wow," Harry said. "I think it straightened out my back."

And with that, Harry simply walked through customs, jumped into his limo, and went out for the remainder of the evening.

Exactly two months later, in early June of '94, we were in Philadelphia. It was raining, so Harry went to find manager Tom Trebelhorn in the visiting manager's office, where he would tape the pregame manager's show for WGN radio.

When Harry found Treb in his office, Treb was talking with Barry Rozner, the *Daily Herald*'s beat reporter at the time. Harry sat and listened for a while, and then the three chatted about baseball and booze.

Suddenly, a strange creaking noise emanated from the corner of the room, where Harry was sitting on a large, glass coffee table. The three of them stopped to listen for just a split-second, trying to figure out what it was. But before they could spring into action, there was a loud crash and the sound of shattering glass.

And there was Harry, submerged beneath the glass, only his arms and legs visible to the human eye. The table obviously didn't hold his weight, and he went flying through the middle of it. Trebelhorn and Rozner quickly came to Harry's aid because this time he couldn't pick himself up. He looked like a turtle that'd been flipped upside down.

Glass was all over the place and Harry was covered with thousands of little shards of glass. But once they picked him up and brushed him off, everyone realized he would walk away unscathed again.

"Boy, you think someone's trying to tell me something this year," Harry said laughing. "This is my fiftieth year in baseball and maybe I'm not supposed to make it through the season.

"Hey, Treb, we could've pinned this on you, too. What a headline that would be, huh? 'Manager Charged with Murder in Coffee-Table Killing.' You need that right now, don't you, Treb?"

"Yeah, that's perfect," said Trebelhorn, whose team had been eliminated from the race by mid-May. "If you die in my office, I'm really a goner. They'll fire me yesterday. But it's not going to happen. You're indestructible, Harry."

After the playoffs in '84, Harry had to be hospitalized. Most people figured his late nights out and poor eating habits had finally caught up to him, but it turned out to be nothing of the sort. The truth is Harry had some internal bleeding because he had been taking so many aspirin a day for so many years after a terrible auto accident in St. Louis in the '60s. So it had nothing to do with his drinking at all. He just had to stop taking so many aspirin.

◆❖◆

One of my favorite Harry stories is the one about that car accident. When he was run over by that car, he broke both his legs, his nose, and his shoulder. Everyone was certain he wouldn't make Opening Day that season.

"Well, Steve," Harry said, "I got rid of the crutches about ten days before Opening Day and the doctors couldn't believe it. I was ready to go. I still needed a cane, but I could get by without it if I had to.

"But on Opening Night, we had about 50,000 people in St. Louis and this was their first chance to see me since the accident. I was on the field introducing the celebrities, and I walked out with the crutches under my arms.

"I got out onto the field and as they let out a big roar, I made a big production out of throwing one of the crutches away. That brought an even bigger roar. So as I got near the mike, I made a gesture as if to say, you've inspired to me try it without any crutches, and I threw the other one away and the crowd went berserk.

"After all that was over, I limped off the field to a standing ovation and as I walked through the Cardinals' dugout, Bob Gibson stopped me and with a quizzical look on his face said, 'Harry, I thought you got rid of the crutches two weeks ago? What was that?' 'Gibby,' I said, 'this is show biz, buddy. You know more about pitching in your little finger than I do in my whole body, but you don't know show biz. This is show business and there's nothing wrong with giving people some entertainment along with the game.' I think I taught Gibby something that day."

Another miraculous recovery was followed by yet another perfect performance.

Harry was always looking out for me and began that task

early in the 1983 season, my first as his partner in the Cubs' broadcast booth.

It was the first week of the season. We were in Cincinnati, which has one of the trickiest booths in the National League because the metal staircase leading down to the front row of the box is steeper than the upper deck at the new Comiskey Park. "Now, Steve," Harry began, "be very careful going down there because you could fall right out of the booth, or break your neck going down those stairs."

It didn't have much of an effect on me because I stayed in the booth for nine innings, while Harry had to move over to radio for the middle three innings and then come back to TV for the final three.

So I was doing OK with the stairs and was busy writing in my scorebook when Harry came back to the TV booth in the top of the seventh. I wasn't paying much attention because, after all, Harry was the one who warned me about the stairs, but suddenly I heard a, "Whoaaaaah!"

I spun around and saw books and papers flying everywhere and there was Harry hanging upside down from the top step, with one foot stuck in a stair, three or four steps above where his head rested against a wall.

His leg was twisted under one of the stairs and the scorebook and notes were strewn all over the booth. But we were only about twenty-five seconds away from going back on the air with a live shot.

So I jumped out of my chair and ran over to untangle Harry. I had to go up the stairs, get past his body and work my way up to where the foot was. These were very sharp, hard, corrugated steel stairs. As I made my way to the scene of the accident I couldn't believe Harry hadn't split his head open. I managed to pry his shoe loose and Harry slowly slid down the rest of the way head first and came to a stop at the bottom of the booth. Harry picked himself up, gathered his papers and scorebook, and did the seventh-inning live shot in the booth as though nothing had occurred.

How, I asked myself, could he not even have one bump or bruise? How could he not have a broken ankle or leg? How could his hair not even be mussed? All I could do was shake my head.

Mandy Cohen was our assistant director in the booth for much of the nineties. One day she wasn't in the booth because she was out of town working a Bulls game, so we had a replacement assistant just for that day.

That was tricky business because we had a screen in the front of the booth that needed to be pulled down on sunny days. That cut down the glare of the backdrop Arne used for the pregame shot from the camera in the back of the booth.

Well, this new kid went to put down the screen, but he couldn't get it to work. He was handling this large metal pole when it came down and struck Harry in the head from behind, which was followed shortly thereafter by the screen, which then entangled Harry.

"Whoaaaaaa!" Harry yelled. "What the hell was that? Is someone trying to kill me?"

Just then, we cut to the live shot and there was Harry stuck inside the screen like a caged ferret. He wasn't real excited about it, and the poor kid looked like he was the one who was going to die.

When we cut to a break, I looked up at the guy and said, "That's a nice career you just had, son. It's been nice talking to you." I could just see the headlines: "Assistant Kills Harry in Freak Accident; WGN Vanishes Guy from Planet." He may still have been on the planet, but we certainly never saw him in the booth again.

Fortunately, Harry came away unscathed. And I wasn't surprised at all. Harry was simply indestructible.

"There's Danger Here, Chéri!"

That was one of Harry's favorite sayings when the Cubs were in trouble in the late innings. But that trouble was nothing compared to that which Harry regularly got himself into in our broadcast booth. His travails were legendary, and at times he nearly took me with him as he tempted fate and even death.

As long as I knew Harry, he never once went to the bathroom during the course of a game. It didn't matter if it was a two-hour, nine-inning game or a five-hour, seventeen-inning game. Harry didn't visit the men's room during the game, so the only thing I could figure is he had a bladder the size of Long Island.

"Harry," I asked him once, "how can you do that?"

"I'll tell you, Steve," Harry chuckled, "I've trained myself never to go until after the last out of any game. While the game is going on, that's all I'm thinking about. But as soon as that game ends, I sprint for the bathroom."

And because of that, Harry would always make a pit stop right before the game began. He had a routine—and an imaginary clock in his head—and he knew when it was time to shuffle over to the bathroom.

That's what he did on one beautiful June day in 1993. He came back from his trip to the washroom, and as he did every day, he proceeded to ask Mandy Cohen if she would get him a root beer.

Well, the fact of the matter is that there wasn't any root beer in the press box lunchroom. There wasn't any that day. There wasn't going to be any the next day. And there wasn't ever going to be any root beer. And every day, Mandy told Harry there wasn't any root beer.

"Harry," she said, "there isn't one press room in the league that has root beer, including Chicago, so why do you ask for it every day?"

But every single day Harry asked for it anyway. "Mandy," Harry would plead, "I need a root beer!"

So every day Mandy would come back with a Diet Coke or a Seven-Up or a glass of water and tell Harry she had his root beer for him. Harry would drink it down like it was the best root beer he'd ever had. Until the last day Mandy ever got Harry a drink, he always asked for a root beer and she always delivered him a drink he really believed was root beer.

And on this particular day in June at Wrigley Field, Mandy left to get Harry a "root beer" while he visited the washroom. Upon returning to the booth, Harry was standing next to me when he discovered that he'd left his zipper open. I was writing out my pregame notes in my scorebook when I heard a blood-curdling scream.

"Whoaaaaaaa!" Harry yelled. "I'm stuck!"

I looked over and there was Chicago's Very Own with his male appendage caught in his zipper. I was stunned by his predicament, but this was one of those few times I left Harry to get himself out of it, so to speak.

Seemingly in a fight for his conjugal life, Harry tugged harder and harder and harder, and kept on yelling, "I'm stuck, I'm stuck, I'm stuck!"

In the meantime, the fans—who can see into our broadcast

booth from the upper deck grandstand—were quickly realizing that something wacky was happening in the booth.

"Harry," I said, trying not to laugh, "you better sit down because people are starting to look in here."

"But I'm stuck!" he yelled. "I'm really stuck!"

Harry was gyrating back and forth like Elvis in one of the most painful situations of his life. With the tears rolling down his face from pain—and down mine from laughter—Harry then sat down and tugged for all he was worth.

Suddenly, Mandy reappeared with his drink, and I leaned over to Harry and whispered, "Harry, you better yank that thing back in because Mandy's back." So Harry gave one mighty tug and with the groan of a thousand men, he extricated himself from the horrible dilemma. Just as Mandy arrived at the desk, Harry had everything back in its proper place.

Mandy took one look at me with tears running down my face and the sick expression on Harry's face and said, "What's going on here? What did I miss?"

"Nothing, Mandy," I said laughing. "Everything's fine."

But once again, Harry had it all together seconds later as we went right into a pregame show and despite the fog in his eyes, he didn't miss a beat. By the time the seventh-inning stretch rolled around, he was as strong as an ox and you would have never known what took place before the game.

Philadelphia had always been a dangerous town for Harry, both in the booth and on the streets, but there was a day in 1986 that was almost his last.

You see, at Veterans Stadium there's a ledge at the front of the booth and it's very low. It comes up to about your knee, but it's sort of important since it's the only wall that separates you from falling thirty feet into the stands.

There's also a platform we stand on so that the camera can get the proper angle on us for the pregame and postgame shows. We also used only one microphone at the time because Harry wanted control of the mike when we went on camera. (After ten years together, Harry finally relented and let me have my own microphone, but that was an honor that yet awaited me.)

On this one day in Philly, Harry decided he was going to stand on the platform and I would stand on the floor so he could put the mike down toward me and make it seem like he was eight inches taller.

Now the fact is, I was two-and-a-half inches taller than Harry was, but to listen to him talk over the years, you know he viewed himself as being a big guy. He'd always say to me, "You short guys can relate to each other. You and Rey Sanchez and Todd Haney, you guys all stick together." And I'd say, "Who are you, Kareem Abdul-Jabbar?"

But as we got closer to going on camera, Harry looked at the potential for disaster—what with the potential thirty-foot fall and all—and decided that the platform wasn't a good idea.

"I'll just step down from here," Harry said, as he began to move. "I don't want to fall."

Sure enough, he stumbled as he tried to get down, which, of course, was just what he was afraid of. To get his balance and save himself, he swung his arm around and hit me with all of his weight—and knocked me right out over the ledge.

As I began to tumble over the side—within an eyelash of falling completely out of the booth to an untimely death at the Vet—I managed to grab onto the wall with one hand.

It still wasn't clear whether I would live to see another day when all of a sudden I heard, "Hello again, everybody. With Steve Stone, this is Harry Caray from Veterans Stadium. . . ."

I was seeing my life flash before my eyes and Harry was introducing us on the air, and this was when we were doing the pregame live, before Harry got too unpredictable and we had to tape them.

So there I was, barely clinging to life. I somehow managed to regain my balance and snapped back into the booth, but my face was red, sweat was pouring down my face, and my heart was pounding out of my chest.

I was certainly in no condition to be on camera, so of course Harry said, "What a beautiful night for baseball, isn't it, Steve?"

And he stuck the mike in my face.

"Yes, Harry," I said, wiping the fear of death off my face. "It's a terrific night." In one instant I was fighting for my life and in the next instant I was trying to speak and sound intelligent about who was pitching that night for the Cubs and Phillies.

That was one of the defining moments in our relationship.

St. Louis was always a great town for Harry. As a broadcaster for many years there, he was a huge star and had many friends in the region.

So during the seventh-inning stretch at Busch Stadium, he'd stand up as they played the Budweiser song and hold up a cup as though he was drinking a Bud.

But on one hot summer night at Busch Stadium in the mid-'90s, Harry had trouble finding his chair all evening. The chairs are on wheels in that booth because they're easier to move. At the end of the seventh-inning stretch, Harry tried to sit down, but hadn't realized how far he'd moved his chair. He missed the chair completely and went down for the count hard. Now this was well past his stroke of 1987 and any time Harry went down, it was cause for concern.

So there he was on the floor of the booth calling for help. The guys on radio, Thom Brennaman and Ron Santo, had witnessed the fall. They were yelling at me to help him up and, of course, laughing at me the whole time. The problem is, I'd had back surgery just a few months prior to that. Despite this,

I bent over put out my left hand and said, "Harry, grab my hand."

He grabbed for it, but I realized I couldn't lift him up because of the back surgery. I was on a thirty-pound limit, which Harry exceeded by at least 200 pounds. As much as I cared for him, I wasn't going to have another back surgery for him. And besides, at that point, he'd never been hurt by any of his falls anyway.

So there I was, as we were about to come out of a commercial, making some half-hearted efforts to lift him up, holding his hand, but not getting anywhere fast. Thom and Ron were laughing hysterically and yelling at me to help him. I was pointing to my back and yelling back about the thirty-pound limit. It was a regular Laurel and Hardy routine.

Finally, moments before we went back on the air, a cameraman, seeing Harry's predicament, ran in and hoisted him up. As usual, Harry came away unscathed and was ready to go when the red light came on.

"Back at Busch Memorial Hospital, Harry Caray and Steve Stone. . ."

The beauty of our booth at Wrigley Field is that in the summer, the warm blissful breezes blow from the southwest, which is from behind home plate. That means that when it's boiling hot and humid, we get absolutely no breeze up there because the stadium blocks the wind.

One night, it was 103 degrees at game time for a 7:05 contest and with the humidity, it felt like 112. They had Harry literally packed in ice from his neck all the way down to his shorts. They had ice in his shirt and ice on his head. It was an unbelievable sight.

The flip side is that when it's cold, the wind comes from the east, straight off of Lake Michigan, right over the center field scoreboard and directly in the WGN-TV booth.

Harry always said he needed to have a feel for the game and a feel for the crowd. That, in turn, meant I would have no feeling in my hands, feet, face, and most of the rest of me, because he insisted on leaving the broadcast booth wide open. No matter how much I pleaded or begged, Harry wouldn't allow windows in our booth.

At Wrigley Field, April meant temperatures as low as 30 degrees. With a hawk wind whipping off the lake—right into our faces—the wind chill could and would hover near zero. If you've ever spent four or five hours outside in Chicago—particularly in the shade—during the first six weeks of the baseball season, then you know it's an endurance test. I felt many days like I was participating in the Iditarod.

One day on the air I said, "Harry, are you sure we can't have the windows in here?"

"No, not a chance, Steve," Harry said with pride. "I gotta have a feel for the game. Whatsamatter? Not tough enough to take it?"

"Absolutely not," I said. "And by the way, your entire face has turned blue and you look like a Smurf. Your teeth are chattering and that brownie you put in your mouth a half-hour ago is still frozen. I know you want to have a feel for the game, but I just want some feeling in my toes."

We truly have the worst of both weather worlds, but the nastiest part of the open-window policy was that Harry would always get a terrible cold when we got to Chicago. Here he had spent the entire winter in the warmth of Palm Springs and Mesa, and now he was in Chicago in an open-air stadium with open-air windows.

So he would inevitably start with this hacking cough early in the season and it would last until the days got warm in late May. This was accompanied by a phenomenal amount of congestion and a landfill's worth of phlegm. Now we have a cough switch in our box. When you press this switch, it kills the microphone so you can cough or clear your throat or sneeze or make whatever ugly noise you have to make, and it doesn't go out over the air. The best part is that once Harry actually learned how to use the cough button, he would press on it, but turn and cough right into my microphone. So every spring, while Harry would cough his lungs out on national TV, Arne Harris would get calls from concerned listeners who thought Harry was spitting vital body parts into the grandstand.

Arne finally said, "Harry, people are worried about you, and I know you'd like to have Steve's mike closed when you hit your mute button, but it doesn't work like that. You have to hit your cough button and cough in the other direction from Steve."

But Harry never changed much about his broadcasting style and he certainly wasn't going to learn a new habit now. Some days the phlegm was so overwhelming that he would try to eject it from his throat while calling a play. He thought if he said it louder, it would just clear his throat.

"There's a line drive and DUNSTON makes the play!" Harry would scream, spewing all the while. People at home never understood the random screaming, especially on routine plays, but then, they didn't realize what was happening in Harry's throat.

As Harry's cold would drag on for weeks and months, I'd say, "Harry, have you thought about some medication?" In most years, he didn't get any. But one year he said, "Steve, I've got these antibiotics, and I take six or seven of them a day, but the cold doesn't get any better."

I said, "Harry, has anyone ever told you that if you drink a

bottle of vodka over the course of the night, that it's not going
to allow the antibiotic to work?"

"You're kidding!" Harry said.

"No," I replied. "It's right there on the bottle. If you drink,
it doesn't work. Maybe that's why you have a cold for two
months every spring."

"Oh," he said. "Maybe you're right."

But like most other things I said, he either didn't believe
me or didn't listen, so he had that cold until the ivy turned
green every year.

One thing I learned early in my career with Harry was that
if there was a major announcement to make, Harry certainly
wanted to be the one to make it. But like the dummy I was, I
sometimes forgot. For instance, there was the time early in the
1990 season when the weather in Chicago was terrible.

At that time we were using only one mike, which could be
tough if it was a morning that Harry decided to have a hot dog
with raw onions for breakfast. Working in a cramped booth
during a rain delay and only one mike while he had the breath
of a prairie dog made it a pretty unpleasant place to be. Because there was no place to run, I tried to combat this affront
to my senses with cigars whenever I could.

Well, on this day in 1990, it was snowing and we obviously
weren't going to play the game. Harry and I were killing time
during the delay as usual when we both heard through our earpieces that the Cubs had finally made a decision. Arne told us
that they were calling the game and it would be played later
that week as part of a double-header beginning at noon.

Now this wasn't exactly Dan Rather getting the news that
John F. Kennedy had been pronounced dead in Dallas. It
was hardly an earth-shattering event, but Harry felt like if he
didn't say it, it wasn't official.

We both heard it, but I happened to be speaking at the time it came through the earpiece, so I finished my thought and then started to say, "Harry, we've just gotten word that the game has been . . ."

Just then, I felt this tremendous blow to my chest. All the air rushed out of me and I couldn't speak anymore. Harry had smacked me as hard as he could with the mike!

Harry then grabbed the mike back as I struggled to regain my breath and screamed, "Ladies and gentlemen, I've just been informed that the game has been canceled and it'll be played Thursday at noon as part of a double-header!"

I figured if he wanted to say it that badly, he could've just told me, not hit me, but that was Harry's way of getting the mike back. That just gave me another reason to beg for a second mike in the booth. It would be much better for me and a lot less dangerous, too. I figured it might even extend my career by a few years.

"The Peplinskis Are Here From . . ."

Harry was constantly getting himself into trouble with his on-air comments, but Arne Harris never got enough credit for getting him into some of that trouble to begin with.

Like on that hot summer day in 1985 when Arne showed a bikini-clad woman in the bleachers five times in the first two innings. Now, this woman happened to be quite healthy, if you know what I mean. She had a phenomenal figure and was sensational looking. And good old Arne kept on showing her until Harry bit.

She was wearing a tiny bikini top and Harry was enjoying the view, as were we all. So when we came back for the top of the third inning, Harry said, "Arne, let's get a shot of that girl again."

But through the earpiece, Arne told Harry the show was over.

"We can't shoot her anymore on the air," Arne said, "because the WGN switchboard is lighting up. People are calling in to complain and I can't keep putting her on TV. I'm gonna get lynched."

And that set Harry off—on the air.

"Boy, oh boy," Harry began, with obvious and utter disgust in his voice. "It has come to my attention that some of you out there take exception to Arne Harris shooting that lovely young woman in the bleachers on this gorgeous day for baseball at Wrigley Field.

"Well, I've got just one thing to tell you: You better lighten up a little bit because the clock's ticking and you never know when it's gonna be over, so you might as well have a little fun with us."

That got him off the subject for a while, but in the seventh inning came a note from a fan which said there was a wedding party in the bleachers and the bride was at the game with about fifty of her friends.

"I wonder," Harry said, "if that beautiful young lady that Arne was showing us earlier is the bride." So Arne showed the woman once again and Harry said, "Well, I looked around in back of her and didn't see any wedding party, and I looked around to the sides of her and there isn't a party of fifty there—and there sure ain't room in front of her! Ah, ha, ha, ha, ha, ha!"

◆❖◆

There's no doubt Harry loved to look at beautiful women, and he wasn't shy about letting everyone know that. But people sometimes read more into that than there really was.

One time he said, "Steve, if I can't look at and admire a beautiful woman, then that would be a terrible thing. I love beauty.

"I love beauty in a song or in a painting or in a sculpture, even though I might not understand it. I like beauty in people. I like the way they look or the way they think. I like to go to clubs and hear piano singers because I admire what they do.

"You know, I wonder if we really appreciate the talent in this country and the wonderful people you've never heard of who are so talented. There is so much out there for people to appreciate. And beautiful women are just one of those things."

Harry also saw beauty in giving plugs to his favorite people, and at the top of his list was his attorney, Jack Barry. He always called him, "Prominent Chicago Attorney, Jack Barry." I don't know if he was prominent before Harry began talking about him, but he sure was by the time Harry finished talking about him.

Well, one day it got a little more complicated than he expected. "Prominent Chicago attorney Jack Barry is at the game with his son today," Harry began. "His son played for Frank Leahy, Jack Barry did, and his son, Jack Barry the third, he has his son here, and that's probably Jack Barry the fourth, and Frank Barry, no Leahy. Barry Leahy and Jack Barry went to Notre Dame and played college football with Barry Leahy, whose son Jack Barry is here with his son today and . . ."

And on and on Harry went about the Jack Barrys, leaving us all in a cloud of Barrys, with no idea which one he was talking about. He went on for about an inning-and-a-half and the whole time Arne was in my earpiece telling me to, "Get him off the Barrys, will you?"

I broke in with a little levity . . . or so I thought. "Harry," I asked. "Would that make Jack Barry the 'elder-Barry'?"

"No!" Harry screamed. "Whadaya talking about! No. No. No. That's Jack Barry Sr., and he passed away! This is my friend Jack Barry and he's Jack Barry, son of . . ."

And there he was, back into the Barrys again. He'd missed my weak attempt at a joke and kept on hammering away at the Barrys. My reward was another inning of Barrys and Arne yelling in my ear to get him off the Barrys. In truth, getting him off the Barrys wasn't the solution.

Harry was generally a lot of fun to be around. But as he got older, naturally, more and more of his friends began to pass away, and he was clearly uncomfortable discussing the topic. And every time someone died, Harry would deliver the eulogy coast-to-coast on WGN-TV.

We were in Los Angeles when Roy Campanella passed away in 1993, and Harry, Don Drysdale, and myself spent several minutes on and off the air telling terrific stories about Campy.

We were in Denver just a few days later when, tragically, we got word that Don Drysdale had passed away in a hotel room in Montreal. Harry announced it on the air and mentioned how we'd just seen Don in L.A.

"It's a very sad day in baseball," Harry said. "It was just a short week ago in L.A. when Don Drysdale was telling all those wonderful vaginettes about Roy Campanella."

Arne went nuts.

"Vaginettes! Vaginettes!" Arne yelled in my ear. "What's he talking about? What the hell are vaginettes?"

"I'm staying out of this one," I told Arne off the air. "If I get involved, I'm the one who'll wind up with an FCC complaint."

Of course, Harry meant vignettes. Harry's heart was often in the right place, but his semantics were sometimes a little haywire.

Another sad moment was when we got the news that legendary *Chicago Tribune* columnist Aaron Gold had passed away. Arne informed us of the news in our earpieces, and Harry nearly went to pieces.

"Aaron's dead?" Harry screamed out onto the air.

Yes, Arne replied in Harry's ear, Aaron Gold is dead.

"Aaron's dead?" Harry said again.

Yes, Arne repeated, Aaron Gold is dead.

"Aaron?" Harry said for third time. "Aaron is dead? I can't believe it."

I'm sorry, Harry, Arne said into his ear, but you have to tell the people who it is. They're only hearing one side of this conversation and Aaron could be anyone. Some people might think it's Henry Aaron.

"Boy, oh boy," Harry said, shaking his head. "Aaron's dead. What a sad day. My goodness."

Harry, Arne said again, would you tell people who it is? Please!

"Everyone knows Aaron," Harry said. "What a terrific guy he was."

Aaron Gold, Harry.

"Yeah, Aaron, what a wonderful man," Harry said. "I can't believe Aaron's gone."

Steve, Arne was pleading now, help him out.

I would've, but I couldn't get a word in edgewise. Finally, Harry took a breath and I mentioned it was Aaron Gold, the famous columnist, and everyone watching finally knew who had passed away.

Sometimes Harry just forgot that the folks at home couldn't hear Arne.

During the 1997 season, Josh Lewin called our games on the road and handled the pregame and postgame duties at home. Josh did everything he could to ingratiate himself to Harry, but Harry really wasn't interested in pursuing that relationship. At that point in his life, I have to believe that Harry felt like Josh was sitting in Chip Caray's chair, even though Chip was not yet interested in taking the job.

So Josh didn't get to call home games, but he did show up every day at Wrigley Field and often tried to make small talk with Harry, hoping he might throw a bone of interest back at him. That rarely happened.

One morning Josh stopped in just after returning from the funeral of his grandmother and decided this might be a good

time to spend a moment with Harry. Josh mentioned his grandmother's passing and said, "Harry, I just want to thank you for
making my grandmother's life enjoyable for the last year or
two. She started watching the Cubs and got hooked on the
team because of you. She watched all the games and she loved
Harry Caray. She thought you were just great. So I just wanted
to thank you for making her life a little more enjoyable."

With that, Lewin stopped, took a breath and waited for
some sort of condolence or acknowledgment. Harry, who to
this point hadn't even looked up from his scorebook, stopped
writing, threw down his pen, leaned back in his chair and
looked out onto the field—without so much as a gaze in
Lewin's direction.

"Yeah, Levine," Harry said to Lewin, "all my fans are
dying."

Harry went back to filling out his scorebook, and Josh
turned around and left the booth.

When Harry would get something in his mind, it was locked
in there forever. And whenever Bill Murray came up to the
booth, Harry would ask about his mom, since the family
grew up in a northern suburb of Chicago and she was a big
Cub fan.

But after Bill's mom passed away, I mentioned it to Harry
so that the next time Bill visited with us, Harry wouldn't ask
about Bill's mom. Sure enough, the next time Bill came up to
the booth, Harry's first words were, "Bill, how's your mom
doing up there in Wilmette?"

"Well, she's dead, Harry," Bill said on the air without changing expression. "And don't ask me about my father, because
he's dead, too."

Whenever we got a note from someone who was approaching triple digits, Harry made that a priority mention.

"Bill Graffanolino turns ninty-five years old tomorrow and he's watching the ball game down in Chattanooga today," Harry would say with a chuckle. "And I thought I better get that one in early, because at his age, you never know."

Harry, Jack Buck, and I were sitting in the lunchroom at Busch Stadium one night before a game in 1993 when Harry actually admitted that he and Jack were getting up there in age.

"No kidding, Harry," Jack said. "When you get to be our age, the only thing you have to look forward to is sitting on the toilet until your legs go numb."

One of the most amazing things about Harry was that—as the world changed and you read more about terrorism and mayhem, and people were getting crazier and crazier—nothing scared him. I, for instance, stopped eating anything that came up to the booth. I mean, you never know where something's coming from and how nuts the people were who were sending it.

The "Nuts on Clark" people, from the terrific store just down the street near the ballpark, are always very nice and send up enough goodies to feed a small country. I eat their products without hesitation. But most of the time we didn't know where this stuff was coming from.

Fans would send up brownies and cakes and pies and corn beef sandwiches and ribs and chicken and anything you can think of. I'm sure they were all wonderful people, but from a safety standpoint I couldn't bring myself to sample anything unless Harry did first.

Indestructible Harry never felt like anyone would do anything to him. I'll tell you what, that man never got sick from anything and he always ate everything. Usually, I'd wait until he took a bite and if he remained upright, I figured it was probably OK.

At times, near the end of his career, he wasn't easy to understand, and he was even tougher to understand when he had a mouth full of Gummi Bears. Harry thought nothing of talking with his mouth full.

The people at home could hear him talking with food in his mouth and I'm sure they wondered what he was munching on, so one day Arne asked him what he was eating. "Arne," Harry said on the air, "the Peplinskis are here from Terre Haute and they brought up some brownies. Arne, you should have some of these."

Of course, Arne was 1,000 feet away in the production truck, so that would've been some trick, but Harry liked to let the people know what he was eating during a game because it made everyone feel like he was broadcasting from their kitchen.

That's the way Harry wanted it, even if it wasn't exactly the way they teach broadcast journalism in college. In fact, that's probably why he did it that way.

But Arne was always so far away that he had no chance to sample whatever it was Harry was teasing him with.

"Steve, does he know where the truck is?" Arne would laugh into my earpiece. "I mean, does he think I'm hiding under his chair? And get him off the brownies already, would you?"

There was no getting Harry off of anything.

When Harry was on radio he mentioned even more names than he did on TV, I guess because there was more time to fill.

"I think reading a guy's name is the greatest thing in the world," Harry told me early in my career. "You say hello to Bobby Jones, who's here today from Spokane, Washington, and he wants to say hello to the guys down at O'Reilly's Tavern. Well, Bobby Jones remembers that forever. And every one of his friends remembers it. And everyone in his family for the next five generations remembers it. And he feels like a million bucks.

"So what's so bad about that? Maybe you make some friends and sell some more tickets and get better ratings. Steve, people will criticize me for that for the rest of my life, but I don't care. I think it's good for all of us."

Harry said it was particularly important after he came back from his stroke.

"When I was in that hospital bed in Palm Springs and I couldn't move my arm and I didn't know how sick I was or when I would be able to return to broadcasting, I read every single letter I got from the fans," Harry said. "And it made me feel so much better. And that's when I understood that if I mentioned a guy recovering in a hospital somewhere, I might be able to encourage him or make him feel better. I know what it's like and I know it makes a difference. I did it before my stroke but I didn't realize what it meant to people until they did it for me after my stroke."

There was one time he read a note in San Francisco that might've been the all-timer. We were at Candlestick Park in 1991 when someone sent up a prank note for Harry to read that said, "The Gerbil family is here from San Francisco."

At the time, Bob Brenly was working with Harry on radio and he happened to see the note in a pile of messages. He knew it was a joke and flipped it up in the air as if to discard it out of the booth.

But sure enough, the swirling winds at the Stick pushed the note back into the booth and it landed right in front of Harry, who was on the air. Before Brenly could grab it back, Harry was pushing Brenly's arm away and studying the message carefully.

He decided to go ahead with the note and read it on the air while it was still fresh in his mind. So he blurted out, "A busload of Gurbers, er rather, Gerbils from downtown San Francisco are here to root for the Cubs today."

Brenly couldn't even speak. He was doubled over with laughter, trying not to make noise on the air. The engineer was falling down with laughter. And Harry just kept on going, never having known the comedy that took place.

And he raised his palms in that usual fashion as if to say, "What'd I do?"

"Steve, Where's He Looking?"

The booth was not only a dangerous place to be with Harry some of the time, but it was also an exciting place to be all of the time.

One reason was the infamous cough switch. You see, we have this cough switch attached to a box about three inches above the counter top where all of our microphones and papers reside.

Well, one day I had my earpiece in and was getting ready to do the tenth-inning postgame show, while I listened to Arne give Harry instructions for the wrap-up.

Now it seems to me that if you were to sit on the cough switch you'd pretty much have to know about it. It's three inches of steel with a half-inch metal button, and somewhere along the line you'd feel that creeping up your backside— unless, of course, you were Harry.

This was 1989 and he was so excited about wrapping up another Cubs victory that he wouldn't have felt it if a "umi-corm" was underneath him. So Harry started to do the postgame show and nothing was coming out of his mike. Arne, meanwhile, was frantically checking to see what might have gone wrong. Complicating matters even more, Harry's ear-piece was rarely in his ear, so Arne couldn't talk to him. Instead, he would talk to me.

"Steve," Arne said, "is he sitting on his cough button?"

I peered down at his posterior and sure enough, all that steel had disappeared beneath him.

"Arne, he's on it all right," I said off the air and through the intercom. "I don't know how he doesn't feel it."

"Do you think you can pull him off the button?" Arne asked. "I can't talk to him because he's lost the earpiece again."

"I'll take a shot, Arne," I said. "But don't get your hopes up."

I tried to make sure my hand wouldn't get in the camera shot, but as I leaned over to get his arm and lift him up, all I got was the wire attached to his earpiece. Now as I'm doing this, I'm watching the TV monitor to see what it looks like on TV at home, and suddenly I see the earpiece come flying across the booth.

"Did you move him?" Arne asked. "I still don't hear anything."

"No, Arne," I laughed. "But I got his earpiece *real* good."

So the only people who heard the wrap-up were Harry and I as he sat on that mute button the entire three minutes.

Harry wore an earpiece made in the early '60s, and he refused to part with it. It never worked very well, so I tried everything I could to get him to buy a new one. Once, I even brought in a wax mold that you can put in your ear and then send it out to a company that builds one specifically for you, but he wouldn't go for it.

Until his dying day, he worked with that old-fashioned earpiece and it rarely stayed in his ear. We even assigned a female assistant to the booth to put in his earplug for him every day.

Even after it was placed in his ear, it usually wound up dangling there for everyone in America to see. He'd also have the volume cranked up so loud that I could hear Arne telling him things through his earpiece, and sometimes you could hear that coming out over the airwaves through my microphone.

When it was out of his ear, he'd say, "Arne, I can't hear you. You're breaking up."

Arne would say, "Is this better? Or is this better?"

"Oh, that's it. That's better, Arne," Harry would say.

Meanwhile, Arne hadn't done anything differently. There was nothing he could do but hope that Harry would put it back in, so Arne pretended to adjust some knobs.

That was the continuing saga of the earpiece, which went on for inning after inning, game after game, and season after season.

Harry kept a little gooseneck lamp on the table just to his left because he never felt like there was enough light in the booth, and he used it to shine on his scorebook even in the middle of a sunny, summer day.

But he would automatically reach for whatever was directly in front of him to start a broadcast, and one afternoon he didn't look to see what he was grabbing. Just as Arne cut live to us in the booth, Harry reached for the mike in front of him and live on TV, there was Harry Caray broadcasting the Chicago Cubs pregame show into a gooseneck lamp.

"Do you think maybe he could grab the mike?" Arne suggested in my ear.

"I don't know, Arne," I said. "Maybe he'd like to try speaking into the fan instead."

"Hey, Harry," Arne said, "I think you ought to grab the mike."

Harry looked down, saw that he was speaking to a lamp, starting laughing, got his mike and picked up where he left off as if America had heard the first minute of his conversation with a light bulb.

But that was Harry. Not only was he impossible to embarrass, he was even harder to rattle.

Back in 1991, we had a road trip that began in Pittsburgh, where we had a booth that was often confusing. The camera at Three Rivers Stadium is in the back of the booth, so we had to turn around away from the field to face the camera to do the pregame and postgame shows.

But there was also a camera in the next booth, which was the camera that the Pirates used for their broadcast. On this particular night I was hooked up to Arne as usual while Harry did the wrap-up, but lo and behold, he was wrapping up to the Pirates' camera in the booth next door. That left WGN viewers with a great shot of Harry's neck and earpiece, which, of course, was dangling from the side of his head far from his ear.

"Where's he looking?" Arne asked calmly. "Does he know he's looking the wrong way? He's looking at left field."

"I don't know," I said. "Maybe he's looking at the camera next door."

"Why do you think he's doing that?" Arne wondered aloud.

"I have no idea," I said.

"Well, can you turn him around?" Arne asked.

"Not without tackling him," I replied.

"Never mind," Arne said. "Let him go."

So Arne cut away from the spectacular ear-shot to a wide shot of the field while Harry finished the wrap-up.

A few days later, we got to Cincinnati and Harry suddenly remembered that the camera in Pittsburgh was in the back of the booth and toward the door. Unfortunately, that was Pittsburgh and we were now in Cincinnati.

So now Harry did the wrap-up in Cincinnati toward the back of the booth, but the camera at Riverfront Stadium is not in the back of the booth. It's toward the front of the booth and to the right-field side. But Harry did the wrap-up to the imaginary camera in back and we got a terrific shot of Harry's other ear and the other side of his face.

"Now where's he looking?" Arne said laughing.

"He's looking at the door, Arne," I said.

"Any idea why he's looking at the door?" Arne wondered.

"I don't have the vaguest idea," I said.

"Can you move him?" Arne asked.

"No," I replied. "Not a chance."

"OK, never mind. Let him go," Arne said.

So Harry did the wrap-up toward the door where there was no camera and Arne went to a wide shot of the field as Harry finished up the road trip talking to a door at Riverfront Stadium.

Whenever we had a guest in the booth, Harry became a better box-out man than Charles Oakley. Instead of having the person between us, which would mean equal access to the interviewee, Harry always had the guest stand to his left. And I'm telling you, Walter Payton couldn't have gotten past him.

He'd stop them there and keep them to his left. That way, Harry was able to do most of the interview, while I sat there looking like an idiot, smiling and nodding like one of those dolls with the bobbing heads.

In any case, one day three lovely young girls from Ohio managed to find their way into our booth in Pittsburgh. They were terrific kids, ranging in age from about five to ten, and they had made the trip all the way to Pittsburgh just to see their beloved Cubs and, most of all, Harry Caray.

It was a small crowd at Three Rivers that night and somehow these little darlings got up into our booth. They brought some Ohio State University hats for Harry and me, but really they wanted to meet Harry. They were clearly in awe of him sitting there with his wavy white hair and coke-bottle glasses when he called them over.

"I won't bite you," Harry bellowed as the oldest girl approached the great legend. "Come on over."

"We're big Cub fans," she said. "And we brought you some hats from Ohio."

Harry graciously smiled at the girls and took the hats, but when he saw they were Ohio State hats, he went ballistic.

"Ohio State!" he screamed, startling the girls. "Ohio State! I haven't liked Ohio State since Bo Schembechler fired Ernie Harwell! I hate Ohio State. I hate Ohio State. What they did to Ernie Harwell is awful and I wouldn't even dream of wearing that hat."

The girls, naturally, had no idea who Bo Schembechler was and certainly didn't know Ernie Harwell. For starters, Bo Schembechler was the ex-Michigan coach, not an Ohio State coach. But even if Bo had some affiliation with Ohio State, it's hard to understand why Harry would be angry with the school. He was no longer affiliated with coaching when—as president of the Detroit Tigers—he fired legendary announcer Ernie Harwell, who happened to be Harry's dear friend.

Well, the scared little girls ran from the booth, leaving behind the two Ohio State hats. Being a native Buckeye myself, Harry gave me both hats and I still have them to show for my night in Pittsburgh when the Great One scared the daylights out of a trio of unsuspecting Cub fans.

I was always happy to see former Notre Dame coach Digger Phelps come up to the booth to talk a little college basketball. He came by occasionally in the early '80s and then a lot more in the late '80s after I introduced Cubs pitcher Jamie Moyer to Digger's daughter, Karen, who wound up marrying the Cubs' left-hander.

Well, Harry had a way of making even the most vociferous people stop in their tracks, though I didn't think he could ever silence Digger, who always had a quip and a quote ready to go.

One day Digger showed up to watch Jamie pitch and Harry lobbed all the usual questions at him about the team and the state of college basketball and so on and so forth.

Then, Digger was quiet for a minute or two while Harry described some game action, and all of a sudden Harry blurts out, "Hey, Digger, you ever bet on basketball?"

Silence.

I've never seen Digger at a loss for words, but here he was on national TV being asked about one of the worst things a coach could be accused of.

Digger was stunned. He stammered for a minute and looked at me and looked at Harry and looked at the camera and said, "Well, uh, no, of course not, Harry. I mean, I may have tossed a few bucks in an office pool or something, but, uh, no. I mean, uh, no, of course not."

"OK, see ya later, buddy. No runs, one hit, a walk, and a couple of men left on base. We go to the bottom of the fourth, Cubs lead the Reds 6-2."

And that was that.

Digger looked like he did the night Danny Ainge hit the shot over Orlando Woolridge. He was as white as a sheet as he walked out of the booth and stumbled like he'd been punched senseless.

I think it was kind of a game with Harry to see whom he could rattle. Usually, it was me. He had a way of asking a question completely out of nowhere if the thought popped into his mind. He just asked whatever came to his stream of consciousness and thought it might be interesting to fans.

That was pure Harry.

Harry was always trying to pull tricks on me, and as smart as he was, there wasn't a lot you could get away with on him. But one thing I used to do to Harry (and Thom Brennaman and Ron Santo, for that matter) was go into the booth early in the morning of a really hot day before anyone arrived, and I'd turn on the heater down by the floor.

Harry would be sitting there for a few hours sweating like a wildebeest before he'd finally say, "Geez, it's hot in here. I can't believe how hot it is. Mandy, is the heater on?" And poor Mandy Cohen would have to come down and turn off the heater under the table.

She would look at me like I was some kind of a cruel and sadistic individual, which was true, but believe me, Harry would have done it to me if he had just thought of it first.

Back in 1983, WGN-TV held a contest and the winner got to do an inning with Harry and me. It was a dream come true for the young man who won, because he was allowed to broadcast a game with his idol, Harry Caray, for his favorite team of all time, the Cubs.

Harry was very gracious as the fellow described how he loved Harry and the Cubs. Harry then said, "I'll tell you what, you do color while Steve steps aside, and then the next inning you can do some play-by-play, and I'll do the color."

Well, it was great. The first half of the inning, the contest winner added whatever he could and he sure knew the players because he was a great Cub fan. And when it was his turn to do play-by-play, the Cubs were down four or five runs, which seemed to be most of the time back then. The Cubs got a couple of hits and the kid was starting to gain his confidence. You could hear it in his voice because he was mimicking Harry.

"Well, Harry," the kid said, "if we can get a couple more hits

and then a walk and a grand slam, we'll be right back in it."
That was something Harry said all the time, but he didn't like
hearing it this time, especially with a guy doing a bad impression of the Great One.

"We?" he screamed. "We? What do you mean 'we,' buddy?
You got a mouse in your pocket? You're here one inning and
it's 'we' already?"

Needless to say, this guy's broadcast career was short-lived,
and this gentleman, like the Cubs, made an early exit from the
inning.

Harry resumed his rightful place behind the mike and the
kid was never heard from again.

Harry rarely got physical with anyone, especially as he got
older, but there were times when he just couldn't help himself.
Like the time at Mile High Stadium in Denver in 1993.

We had a very nice, but overly ambitious assistant in the
booth there. He had long, blond hair, and long hair was something Harry never approved of on a man.

"Did your barber die?" Harry asked as he saw the kid for
the first time. "Need five bucks for a haircut?"

Things deteriorated from there.

It was the first trip into an expansion city and everyone was
excited, so that meant a lot of interviews for Harry. Every
newspaper, TV, and radio reporter in town wanted to interview
Harry, and he accommodated every single one of them. Harry
was always one for publicity because he had a good sense for
promoting himself and the game of baseball, not to mention
the Cubs and Chicago.

Well, this one TV interview was getting lengthy and we
were getting very close to game time. The assistant didn't realize that Arne took care of everything and only Arne was the
one who decided when and what we did. He's the one who

would inform Harry when it was time to cut the interview off and get to work.

So the assistant really had no responsibilities, but the guy kept saying to Harry, "Speed it up, Harry. We need to get this reporter out of here." He got very close to Harry a couple of times and was obviously aggravating him. Finally, the kid reached down and tried to take the equipment from the TV cameraman and push him out of the booth.

And Harry went nuts.

He reached across two people and punched the kid in the arm!

"I'll tell you when it's time for the interview to be over," Harry yelled. "We'll get to the game, but right now these people are interviewing me, so get the hell away from me and don't come near me again."

Even in 1998, our longhaired former assistant in the booth, who is still doing TV in Denver, was telling the story of being punched by Harry Caray at Mile High Stadium.

Sanderson to Sundberg to Sandberg

Since it was in Harry's nature to go against the grain, he absolutely basked in the glow of inventing new words and phrases. For example, instead of saying a player "hit for the cycle," Harry would say he was "riding the scale." And then, he'd sing the music scale: do, re, mi, fa, sol, la, ti, do.

I'd say, "Harry, it's the cycle, not the scale."

"Well, I like it that way," he said. "How do you know for sure?"

"Well, show me in the media guide where it mentions the last guy who rode the scale," I said. "It does, however, list the last player to hit for the cycle."

"Oh," he said. "That's a good point, but I still like it the other way."

Eventually, he changed to my way of thinking on that one, but it was one of the few victories I ever had in a discussion with Harry. Out of 10,000, about 9,997 went the other way.

There was a day in 1990 when Shawon Dunston had to miss a game because of a groin injury, so I informed Harry of that before the contest and he thanked me for the tip.

But once the game started, he repeatedly said that Dunston was "day-to-day with a hamstring injury." So I quickly scribbled out "groin" on a piece of paper and quietly slid it over to him. But again, he said Dunston was suffering from a hamstring problem.

After the inning was over, I said, "Harry, it's a groin injury. I know because I talked to the trainers before the game."

"You're right, Steve," Harry said, "but I really like to say 'hamstring.' I like that word better."

Every once in a while, Harry would see a big man out on the field, especially the mound, and on the air he'd say, "Steve, how big is this guy?"

"Well, Harry," I'd say, "the media guide lists him at 6-foot-3, 215 pounds." Moments later Harry would go on the air and say, "He's a harse (horse) of a man, about 6-foot-6, 245 pounds." And I'd just look at him and laugh and he would look back at me and put his palms up as if to say, "What did I do wrong?"

Whatever he wanted it to be, became Harry's reality. There was reality and there was Harry's reality. Whatever he thought it was or thought it should be, that's what it was.

Harry had many favorite phrases, such as:

"He's too big to be a man and too small to be a harse."

"There's danger here, Chéri!"

"The big possum walks late." That meant the good team would rally in the end.

"Miss Mesa is here today," or Miss Chicago or Miss Houston or Miss San Diego. Whenever he saw a pretty girl walk through the stands and Arne captured her on TV, that's what Harry would say.

"It's summer resort weather in Chicago."

"You can't beat fun at the old ballpark."

"Boy, oh boy. Budweiser. How can they make it so cheap and have it taste so good?"

"Anyone that tells you that you can have as much fun sober as you can drinking is lying to you."

"He's got a big No. 40 on his back." Or whatever number the pitcher was wearing that day.

"He defies all superstition by wearing No. 13."

"It's a picture-postcard shot." That was for any shot Arne got at Wrigley Field.

"The sky is an azure blue today."

"They're here from Cedar Falls, Iowa."

"Now here's a guy . . ." began any sentence about anyone.

"The beer is colder and the food tastes better when the Cubs win."

"Gaaaaaaad. How can you swing at a pitch that far out-side? You couldn't hit that with a telephone pole."

Nothing got as much reaction as did the spelling of names backward, which was simply a gimmick to kill time and enter-tain fans. Harry told me it began in the late '70s when he and Jimmy Piersall were incredibly bored and someone sent up a note with a long Polish name. Harry had so much trouble pro-nouncing it that he said, "This one might be easier to say backwards." And he did, and that was how it was invented.

A lot of Harry's on-air antics were just that: antics. Like, "Come out from under the table, Steve, I'll protect you," on every single foul ball back near the booth.

I actually caught about a ball a year on the road, and every time he'd grab it out of my hand, show it to the fans and then throw it down to some youngster who would love Harry forev-er. Then, he'd complain about not having his net with him.

Meanwhile, Harry moved with all of the grace of a two-legged elephant in heat, so while I may have been under the table a time or two, Harry sure didn't do much to protect me. Still, it made for some good yucks and some entertaining TV talk.

He would add an "s" to every name that didn't need one, like John Kruks, and take an "s" off of so many that did need them, like the Cub, Dodger, and Brave.

If a guy was from Chicago, like Marvell Wynne, then he wasn't just a ball player on the San Diego Padres. He was "Marvell Wynne from Hirsch High School in Chicago." And if it was someone he liked a lot, like Randy Myers—excuse me, Myer—then it was "Randy Myer from Vancouver, Washington," and every time he saved a game, "They are dancing in the streets of Vancouver, Washington."

Harry was thrilled when Kevin Roberson was called up in 1993, because Roberson was from Decatur. That made for an easy transition from Kevin—every time he was mentioned—to "Decatur, the home of Bob Skeffington, our fine Budweiser distributor." And that was often followed up by a plug for "Don Niestrom of River North Distributing." That way Harry could get in a plug for his friends and a plug for Budweiser.

And if there was any way he could bring up the name of longtime pal and Anheuser-Busch executive Mike Roarty, that meant not only a plug for his buddy, but more airtime for Budweiser.

What a beautiful thing.

And I was thinking of Harry when I announced on WGN that I had written this book, and I just happened to pick our Labor Day telecast in 1998 when the Cubs and Sammy Sosa were facing the Cardinals and Mark McGwire in St. Louis. McGwire blasted No. 61 that day and WGN compiled its highest TV ratings of the season up to that point.

Chip Caray and I discussed the book for a few minutes, and after the inning ended I hit the button to speak directly to Arne and said, "Only Harry could truly appreciate the blatant commercialism of that plug."

Harry never got on a guy for dropping a pop fly in the sun, unless the guy was of Latin descent. "He'd never drop one of those in a million years. Ahhhhhhhhhhh! He did drop it. Holy cow. The guy's from Puerto Rico, where the sun shines every day of the year. How can he lose a ball in the sun?"

And of course, there was the trademark, "There's a long drive. Way back. It might be, it could be, IT IS! Holy Cow! Cubs win, Cubs win, Cubs win! Holy Cow! LISTEN to this crowd."

The only problem was that Harry was the first to admit he couldn't follow the ball all that well the last few years, and if he wasn't watching on the monitor, which he hated to do, then the ball was rattling around in the bleachers by the time he said "it might be." The fans were on the train by the time he said "it could be," and they were home eating dinner by the time he finally got around to "IT IS."

But that was funny, too. Harry told me he would laugh when he watched the highlights at night, because it seemed like everyone in the park knew it was gone before he did.

Despite all of his bravado, much of which was an act, Harry was the first one to poke fun at himself and laugh at a good joke. He also told me that when he first began that home run call, part of the reason he waited so long was that he wanted to let the play happen before he made the call. He didn't want to spoil the suspense for the fan watching the game or listening in the car.

And every time I think of any of these things, I just think about what a great entertainer he was, and how no one will ever come up with an act like this again.

As for the "Holy Cow," Harry said it was simply a way for him to avoid saying a swear word. "In the neighborhood I came from, there was a lot of profanity, so I said 'Holy Cow' instead of 'Holy bleep,' if you know what I mean."

And Harry would only chuckle when someone suggested that Yankees broadcaster Phil Rizzutto used it first.

"Nothing against Phil," Harry said. "But, Steve, for gosh sakes, Phil was playing shortstop for the Yankees until 1956, when I was already saying it on the air since 1945 when I started with the Cardinals.

"So if Phil was saying it, he was saying it on the field to Billy Martin and Jerry Coleman and Bill Skowron and Joe Collins and Yogi Berra, and I was broadcasting it to about forty states."

Harry once admitted that he sometimes mispronounced names on purpose, especially when there was nothing happening in the game. But he also freely admitted that he was never very good at pronouncing names, especially if they had any Latin flavor, because he wasn't well educated. Harry learned life's lessons on the streets of St. Louis, and anything he brought to the broadcast was a product of what he knew or didn't know.

But we did have fun with the names. Sometimes, Harry, Arne, and I were laughing so hard or so mixed up that we couldn't even say a word.

Here are some of my favorite memories:

There was the day in spring training of '93 when the Cubs' Frank Castillo was pitching against the Rockies' Vinny Castilla and Pedro Castellano. "Are you kidding me?" Harry said, laughing when he saw the lineups. "They did this to me on purpose." Needless to say, there was a bit of confusion that day.

But that was nothing compared to what occurred during the 1987 and '88 seasons at Wrigley Field, when we had Scott Sanderson pitching, Jim Sundberg catching, and Ryne Sandberg playing second base. And when they were all in the same game on the same field in the same uniform, Harry really struggled.

Anything could happen, and no one at home really knew what was happening. Sometimes Harry had Sundberg pitching and Sandberg catching and Sanderson fielding balls in the infield. And if you were listening on the radio, forget about it. You had no chance at all.

Sometimes it was "Syne Randberg."

"You had to laugh," Sandberg once told me. "That was funny stuff. I mean, everyone knew what he meant, so what was the harm? All I know is, Harry and I came in with the Cubs at the same time and we spent a lot of years together. He made it fun for everyone, including the players.

"Harry saw me play every game I ever played, except when he was sick. We started with the Cubs [in 1982] at the same time. And he stood up and spoke at 'Ryne Sandberg Day' in 1997, which I thought was a great honor.

"He was always in my corner, for whatever reason, and I appreciated that a lot. I never asked him why, but he seemed to like the way I played the game. It always made me feel good to know that."

Harry and Ryno were linked in other ways, though it may not have been obvious to the naked eye. Both joined the club in 1982, when the Cubs were nothing more than a punching bag for every comedian needing a punchline. And contrary to popular belief, the Cubs never once drew two million people to Wrigley Field until Ryno's MVP season of 1984.

After that, it was an annual occurrence as Sandberg grew into the most popular player in the team's history and Harry emerged as a national icon and an international treasure. Those two, along with the emergence of the satellite and

WGN's superstation, brought the Cubs into a national focus, where they've remained ever since.

Not to take anything away from the original Mr. Cub, Ernie Banks, but as his generation of players and fans faded, Harry and Ryno built a new following that has made the Cubs one of the most influential and popular sports franchises in the world.

Harry never bragged about that, but I think deep down he knew he was at least 33 percent responsible for the rebirth of America's most lovable baseball team.

In 1997, Michael Jordan visited Wrigley Field and Cubs officials went to his skybox to ask him if he wanted to come up to the booth and spend a few minutes with Harry, who absolutely adored Michael.

"No way," Mike said. "I can't do it."

"Why not?" asked a befuddled Cubs official.

"I love Harry," Michael said, "but I don't want to go on the air and have him introduce me as Michael Jackson."

Harry had a lot of fun near the end of the 1986 season when the Cubs called up a twenty-year-old by the name of Greg Maddux. On September 29, Greg faced his brother Mike in the first match-up of rookie starters in major league baseball history.

The fact that Greg beat Mike was nowhere near as important as the match-up in our booth, where Harry was just plain overmatched. It was like Mike Tyson against Mother Theresa.

Harry had Mike pitching for the Cubs half the time and Greg pitching for the Phillies—until they both began to play the outfield. That's because the Cubs had Gary Matthews in left field and the Phils had Garry Maddox in center, and they switched teams a few times themselves.

Harry and I traded punch lines during this 1985 publicity shoot at Wrigley Field. Harry was also pointing out the size of my filthy, stinking cigars. (Courtesy of Steve Stone)

Here's Harry (*left*) and son Skip broadcasting together in St. Louis in 1966. Harry often tried to get his son and grandson to come work with him, but like Harry, they wanted to make it on their own. (Associated Press)

Harry shows off his body while he broadcasts from the bleachers at Comiskey Park in July 1973. He carried on the tradition of calling a game with the fans when he moved north to Wrigley Field in 1982. (Associated Press)

Harry Caray leans out of the old WGN broadcast booth to lead the crowd in singing "Take Me Out to the Ball Game" during the seventh-inning stretch. Jack Rosenberg and I look on during this September 1984 game at Wrigley Field. (Associated Press)

A jubilant Harry returns to the booth on May 19, 1987, for the first time since suffering a stroke on February 17. Harry had good reason to be all smiles as his favorite pitcher, Rick Sutcliffe, defeated the Reds 9–2. Ed Lynch, who is now the general manager of the Cubs, collected the save. (Associated Press)

President Ronald Reagan joins Harry in the booth during a surprise visit to Wrigley Field on September 30, 1988. That was one of the few times Harry stepped aside and let someone else call the action. (Associated Press)

At the Baseball Hall of
Fame in Cooperstown, New
York, Harry receives the
Ford C. Frick Award from
Hall of Famer Ralph Kiner
in 1989. (Associated Press)

St. Louis Cardinals coach Red Schoendienst shares a moment with Harry prior
to a Cardinals-Cubs game at Busch Stadium. Both men were inducted into the
Baseball Hall of Fame two days earlier on July 23, 1989. (Associated Press)

Three generations of Carays prepare to make history by lunching at Harry Caray's restaurant in downtown Chicago on May 13, 1991. A few hours later, son Skip (*right*) and grandson Chip (*left*) would bring Harry's dream to fruition as the three men broadcast a Cubs-Braves game together. Skip has been the voice of the Braves for twenty-four years, while Chip is now the No. 1 man in Chicago. (Associated Press)

Arne Harris (*left*), Harry, and I take a break from our arduous spring training duties in Mesa, Arizona. (Courtesy of Arne Harris)

Harry Caray steps up to the plate at Wrigley Field with sports announcer Bob Costas for a 1994 tribute, "When Harry Met Baseball," honoring Harry's fifty years in broadcasting. (Courtesy of WGN-TV)

Harry poses with two of his favorite people in the whole world. In the middle is 1984 Cy Young Award winner Rick Sutcliffe and on the right is award-winning WGN legend Arne Harris. (Courtesy of Arne Harris)

Harry always took time out of his day to sign autographs for the fans. He believed that without them he never would have succeeded, and he always tried to remember the great Cub fans. (Courtesy of Steve Stone)

As was usually the case, Harry got the better part of the deal as we posed for a picture during a WGN-TV gala in 1988. Harry always drew an attractive crowd, and this particular evening was no exception. (Courtesy of Steve Stone)

As you can see from this photo, the fans could easily view the events taking place in our broadcast booth at Wrigley Field. In this case, Harry was merely toasting another beautiful day at the ballpark, but our moments in the booth weren't always that serene. (Courtesy of Steve Stone)

With no baseball to broadcast because of the strike in the late summer of 1994, Harry passes the time by taking part in the Schaumburg Septemberfest Parade in suburban Chicago. If Harry wasn't drawing a crowd, he certainly knew where to find one. (Dan White/Daily Herald)

Longtime pals and previous inductees Harry Caray and Jack Brickhouse spend a moment together on Oct. 29, 1995, at the Museum of Broadcast Communications' Radio Hall of Fame ceremonies. Both Chicago legends died in 1998, leaving Cub fans without two of the greatest who ever lived. (Associated Press)

As Cubs marketing director John McDonough looks on in the background, Harry prepares to throw out "the first pitch" at the Cubs Convention in 1996. Harry was one of the big reasons the convention sold out every January in Chicago. (Associated Press)

Harry interviews Cubs second baseman Ryne Sandberg before a spring training game against the Milwaukee Brewers in Mesa, Arizona, in March 1996. It was Harry's fifty-second year in baseball broadcasting and Sandberg's return to the game as a player after twenty months in retirement. No one was happier than Harry that "Ryno" was back.
(Associated Press)

No one knew it on September 21, 1997, but this was Harry leading the crowd during the seventh-inning stretch for the very last time at Wrigley Field.
(Chris Hankins/Daily Herald)

Harry shares a laugh with Cubs first baseman Mark Grace at the 1998 Cubs Convention. Harry looked like the picture of health on January 16, 1998, but he died thirty-three days after this photo was taken.
(Mark Welsh/Daily Herald)

The crowd at the 1998 Cubs Convention joins Harry in a boisterous rendition of "Take Me Out to the Ball Game." This was his final serenade to Cub fans—on this planet, anyway. (Mark Welsh/Daily Herald)

On February 19, 1998, the day after Harry's death, fans leave
mementos of candles, beer bottles, and Cubs paraphernalia on
the Harry Caray tile in the Walk of Fame outside Wrigley Field.
(Associated Press)

Harry's grandchildren serve
as pallbearers as his coffin is
carried out of Holy Name
Cathedral to the strains of
"Take Me Out to the Ball
Game," bellowed out by the
church's beautiful pipe organ.
(Mark Welsh/Daily Herald)

The guest conductor series was a big hit in 1998, but it was never more emotional than on April 3, when Dutchie Caray led the adoring crowd during the seventh-inning stretch on Opening Day at Wrigley Field. It set the tone for a magical season at the Friendly Confines. (Bob Chwedyk/Daily Herald)

It got worse in the late '80s when St. Louis brought up a hurler named Greg Mathews. The Cards also didn't do Harry any favors in 1995 when they brought in T.J. Mathews, who in one game was "O.J. Maddux," "T.J. Maddox," and "Gary Mathews."

Whenever Harry saw a player for the first time, he'd ask me how to pronounce his name. One time he pointed to the name of Rafael Belliard and asked for some help. I told him, but it didn't make any difference.

"Rafer, uh, Rafat, uh, Rafael Bellardo," Harry stammered. "Wait, uh, Rafael Belliard."

"That's it," I shouted. "By Joe, Harry, I think you've got it."

And so he finally had it. Until, of course, the game started. The first ground ball went to the shortstop and Harry said, "There's a routine grounder to Bellardo . . ." and so went the entire series. On Belliard's next trip to Chicago, the first ball in the bottom of the first was also hit to "Bellardo," but as he went to backhand the ball, he broke his left leg and Harry was done with Bellardo, I mean Belliard, for the season.

"Wow," Harry said when he heard the news. "That's really bad for him . . . but really good for me."

Harry didn't get that lucky when the Cubs called up a portly catcher by the name of Hector Villanueva in 1990. Once again we went through our drill of me writing it out phonetically for him and then him mispronouncing it for an hour before the game began.

The first day he tried it, he threw seven different versions at WGN viewers. There was Valenzuela, Velezuela, Venezuela, Villanova, Villaneva, Villanuega, and Villanezuela.

Harry looked at his score sheet with the phonetic spelling, looked at me and then said, "Here comes Hector to bat for the second time today."

And from that moment on, he was known only as Hector.

He took the same tact when we first ran into the Expos' Mark Grudzielanek. Harry took one look at it, thought about spelling it backward, and said on the air, "Steve, it looks like it's already spelled backward, or maybe sideways."

After a few trips to the plate and several "Gruzzulniaks," Harry decided he would say, "All of his teammates refer to him as Mark G," and that's what Harry did from that point forward. That fell into the category of Harry's reality.

The Cubs had a great, young, up-and-coming superstar named Rafael Palmeiro in the late '80s, but Harry insisted his name was "Palermo." I heard it said that way so many times that I found myself analyzing a replay in Pittsburgh one night, and I said, "There you see the drive going over Palermo's head."

"Ah-hah!" Harry yelled. "See, it's not so goddamn easy, is it?"

In this case, Harry's reality had become part of my consciousness.

At the annual WGN sponsor's banquet in Arizona in the spring of '89, Harry did his usual fabulous job as emcee. But after a very flowery introduction of general manager Jim Frey, Harry stunned everyone by saying, "I just have one question: How in the hell could you trade Rafael Palmeiro?"

Frey, who had a very caustic wit himself, replied, "Harry, I just got sick and tired of hearing you call him Palermo every day."

At the same banquet in 1996, Harry introduced manager Jim Riggleman as famous restaurateur "Jimmy Rittenberg." At which point Riggleman took the mike and said, "Thanks, Hank."

On Opening Day 1997, Chris O'Donnell visited our booth after throwing out the first pitch. He was sort of sitting there waiting for Harry to interview him, as was the custom for the first-pitch person, when Harry finally looked over at him and said, "So, Chris, what are doing with yourself these days?"

"Well, Harry," Chris said, seemingly surprised that Harry hadn't studied his bio, "I just made a 'Batman' movie and I played Robin, and I'm working on some other films and things are going very well. But you know, Harry, more important than that is my dad's here in the booth and he's a big fan of yours and . . ."

"Oh yeah," Harry interrupted. "I've known your dad for years. How ya doin', Bud?"

"Fine, Harry," he replied. "But my name's Bill."

In 1997, we were in Los Angeles and Harry was trying to say Chan Ho Park, but it came out Shang Hai Shek. "Harry," I said, "you might be thinking of Chiang Kai Shek. He was not a real nice guy. This guy's a pitcher, Chan Ho Park. He's a pretty nice guy."

"Well," he said. "It sounds like the same thing to me."

Then, he called him "Ho Park" the rest of the night.

When Delino DeShields first appeared on the scene in Montreal, Harry called him "Delino DeSanders." "No, Harry," I said. "You're thinking of Colonel DeSanders, the chicken guy. Or maybe Deion Sanders. But this is Delino DeShields."

Brooks Kieschnick was called "Bryan Kleenex," but that

put him in good company, though not as politically incorrect as when Harry called George Bell "George Bush," or when he referred to Andre Dawson as "Andrew Jackson." Dawson also appeared as "Andrew Dunston," "Andre Dunston," and "Andre Rogers."

When he called Jeff Parrett "Harold," I asked him why. "I don't know," Harry said. "It just seems to go together better than Jeff."

"But that's his name," I said.

"I don't care," Harry said. "It doesn't sound right."

He stunned me in Los Angeles when he called Eddie Murray "Sol Murray," but I knew that at some point in his life he must have known a Sol Murray, and that was the name that came to mind. Eddie also came to be known as "Eddie Murphy," "Eddie Mumphrey," and "Jerry Murray."

Eric Karros was called "Alex Karris," and Damon Berryhill was any number of people, like "Damon Berryman," "Damon Berryhorn," and "Darrin Berryhill."

Even broadcast partner Wayne Larrivee opened a contest once as "Wayne Lassiter."

One of my all-time favorites was Harry calling Cubs media relations director Sharon Pannazzo by the handle of "Sharon Pagnozzi." We didn't even have to be playing the Cardinals for him to do that.

Then there's the case of one Howard Johnson, whose nickname was "HoJo," but Harry couldn't leave it at that. He had to call him "HoJo Johnson." That seemed a bit redundant to me, but it didn't end there. He was also "HoJay Johnson"

around the time of the O.J. Simpson trial. One afternoon on the radio right after he heard the commercial for Lojack, he called him "HoJack Johnson."

You'd think I could escape being victimized since I was his partner for an eternity, but nothing was further from the truth.

He once opened a live broadcast by saying, "Along with Ben Stein, this is Harry Caray at Wrigley Field."

He also used "Ben Stone" a few times and one day we began with him saying, "With Ben Stein, or rather Dave Stone, oh, what the heck's your name again?"

"Steve," I said. "It's been Steve all these years Harry and I swear I haven't changed it."

"Oh yeah," he said. "That's right."

But he never corrected himself on that one.

Whenever the great Paul Hornung came by to say hello, he kept the tradition alive by calling me "Bill" on the air. One time I said, "My name used to be Bill, Paul, but now it's Steve." I guess with Harry referring to me as Ben and Dave (and probably Ben and Jerry's), Harry's friends probably figured it didn't much matter what they called me, and they would have been right.

A question I frequently heard was, "Why don't you correct Harry when he makes a mistake like that?"

Well, it's because Harry knew what he was trying to say and the people at home knew what he was trying to say. It's not as though he didn't know who it really was and everyone knew whom he was talking about.

For me to interrupt the flow of the game and correct him didn't make much sense. Sometimes I would wait a minute or two and say it the right way if I felt like it might need a little clarification. For example, Harry was reading the list of strike-out leaders one day and when he got to "Andy Benes (S.D.)," he said the pitcher was from "South Dakota." About a minute later, I said, "Benes, of San Diego," and worked it into a sentence without embarrassing Harry. There was no need for that, and more times than not, I just let it slide.

Harry earned the right over his Hall of Fame career to be able to make mistakes. What Harry brought to the broadcast was opinion, views, excitement, and a love of the game. That far outweighed the occasional malapropism or miscue.

In the end, it truly didn't matter. People knew what he meant to say and eventually we would get it right, so what did it matter? No one was harmed because Harry said Andy Benes pitched for South Dakota.

Harry had a way of taking the bat right out my hands, so to speak, and it was as easy as saying these two words: "Now ready . . ."

But it wasn't just the words. It was the way he said them and the times that he said them. Sometimes he said that phrase just because he couldn't think of anything else to say before the pitcher delivered a pitch. That was: "Now ready . . . here's the pitch."

But other times he said it just to keep me off the air, and after he delivered it, there was nothing I could do. I had to wait and see where he was going after that before I could do anything.

Another was: "Ry-an Sand-berg . . ." or, "Sam-my So-sa . . ." It would come out of nowhere and just float off into never-never land. He would say a player's name, but that was all. I would sit and wait to see where he was going with it, and often it went nowhere. Sometimes there was more to the story and sometimes it would just fade into thin air.

Harry did most of the talking on our broadcasts. At first it frustrated me because I was trying to establish myself as a color man. But it got to a point where I just sat back and let Harry dictate where we would go and when we would go there.

It got worse, though, when Harry didn't travel anymore, because all of the words he saved up while we were on the road came cascading out when we got home. It was like a trash compactor that kept pushing down the words while we were on the road, and when we got back to Wrigley Field, Harry couldn't stop talking.

I got in about one sentence every half-inning the first few days home after a road trip, and I knew I would have to do most of my talking on the road.

"You know, Steve," Harry joked early in the '97 season, "I just realized that I'm only calling home games and I'm getting older every day. I don't know how many words I have left in me, so I better use them all now."

"Harry," I said laughing, "you talk all you want. I'll just hang around for the fresh air."

Thom Brennaman and I worked together for six years. For most of that time he did the first and last three innings on radio, and the middle three innings on TV with me, while Harry did just the opposite.

I thought I did my best broadcasting during the Harry Caray era with Thom, and from a sheer quantity of words standpoint, there was no contest. I could even talk without Thom raising his hand at me like Harry did when he had something he needed to say and he wanted me to stop in the middle of a thought.

So it was stunning to me when an elderly woman came up to me during spring training 1996 and said she wanted me to do her a favor.

"Hey, why don't you let Harry talk sometimes?" she said

with a straight face. "All I hear is you talk, talk, talk." It was like she had punched me in the sternum and knocked the wind out of me. When I regained my composure, I asked her a question.

"What broadcast are you listening to?" I said with a chuckle. "It can't be the Cubs on WGN because 80 percent of the game is Harry. Go home and put on your VCR and use a stopwatch to time the broadcast. If I spoke any less, I wouldn't even be on the air."

But that's how popular Harry was. People wouldn't have cared if the Beatles were sitting next to him. They wanted to hear Harry talk and I understood that very well.

With most broadcasts you have a play-by-play guy calling the action and when it comes time for the replay, the analyst analyzes the replay. But with Harry and me, Arne would have to show it four or five times so I'd get a chance to say something. Harry would gladly give me the routine grounders to short, but if it was an exciting play, Harry wanted to talk about it on the replay.

For him, there was no division of color man and play-by-play man. There was only: 1) when Harry talked, and 2) when Harry ran out of breath.

Some days we conversed and it led to great conversation, but some days it was Harry talking to the world and it left me talking to myself. Harry always said that was my strong suit anyway.

See No Evil, Hear No Evil, Speak No Evil . . .

Over the years, all of Harry's senses became a little desensitized, and he had a little trouble on the air from time to time.

Like the afternoon at Wrigley Field in 1996 when Harry, Wayne Larrivee, and I were doing the pregame introduction live when suddenly there was a noise and the sounds of several young children singing an unmistakable song down on the field.

"Hey," Harry said as the camera focused on him. "What are they singing?"

"I believe," Wayne said diplomatically, as the camera went to him, "that's our National Anthem, Harry." And as the camera finally made its way to me, now twenty seconds into the song, all I could do was nod, look really stupid, and say, "Our National Anthem."

As you already know, Harry would read just about any note on the air if it meant he could mention Budweiser. But there was a day in April 1997 when such a note almost got him in trouble.

"Hey, Dave and Busters, the great tavern, has a group of 300 here today," Harry said. "Hey, Arne, show the bleachers, will ya?"

It was about 7 below with the wind-chill and Arne was telling me in my earpiece, "Can you get him off of this? There's no one out there." But Harry kept insisting that Arne cut to the bleachers.

"Can't help you, Arne," I said, bailing out. "You're on your own this time."

"Hey, Arne," Harry yelled again. "Show the bleachers. I want to see that group of 300 out in right field, where they must be drinking a lot of Budweiser."

So Arne cut to the right field bleachers, where there were six guys and one girl freezing to death.

"Whadabada," Harry mumbled with disappointment, before saving the plug. "Hey, I'll bet they're all over at Murphy's Bleacher bar behind center field having a lot of Budweiser and staying warm."

Harry wasn't the biggest hockey fan who ever lived, but he did broadcast hockey in St. Louis in the '40s and he liked the sport immensely. It's just that he never got much of a chance to see it in his later years. But he must have done a promo or a commercial for Fox's coverage of the NHL in the spring of '96, because out of nowhere he started talking about hockey every day for a week.

One day Frank Castillo stopped a hard grounder through the box with his foot, and Harry screamed, "Hey, he must have been a hockey goalie when he was growing up. Did you see that?"

"Yeah, Harry," I said. "You see a lot of hockey goalies come from that hotbed of hockey, El Paso, Texas. I'll bet Frankie played a lot of hockey."

And then one night when things were pretty slow, he screamed, "Wow! What an upset! Florida . . . has . . . beaten . . . Philadelphia!"

And at that moment we all scrambled to find our standings to see why a Marlins' victory over the Phillies in May would be so dramatic. But before anyone could figure it out, Harry went on.

"What an incredible story!" Harry yelled. "Now the Flyers . . .are going to be . . . playing in the Stanley Bowl."

"Oh, hockey!" Arne screamed in my ear. "I had no idea where he was going. Get him off the hockey!"

But I was even more confused. It was the Panthers who had upset the Flyers, but they weren't in the Finals yet and, needless to say, it was the Stanley Cup, not a Bowl.

"Where's he going here?" Arne asked.

"I haven't a clue," I said to Arne. "I'm sitting this one out."

And then the next day, he started ranting and raving about a great man who everyone disliked. "Everybody says he's a terrible coach and that the players hate him and the media hates him and the fans hate him," Harry said. "Well, let me ask you a question, Steve."

"Sure, Harry," I said. "But who are you talking about?"

"All he does is win, Steve," Harry responded. "Why does everyone hate him so much?"

"Who, Harry?" I asked again. "Who does everyone hate?"

"I just don't understand," Harry said. "Now here's a guy . . ."

And off he went again, with Arne screaming in my ear, trying to find out whom he was talking about. Finally, it became apparent that it was the infamous Mike Keenan.

"Oh, my God," Arne said in my ear. "What is it with him and the hockey lately?"

"Just a phase," I said. "It'll pass."

And it did.

◆❖◆

Before Cecil Fielder went to Japan and returned to have great success in the States, there was a player named Terry Whitfield in Los Angeles in the mid-'80s trying to accomplish the same thing. Whitfield had left the Giants about five years before and come back to play for the Dodgers.

It was a unique story at the time and I was detailing it on the air one night in Los Angeles when Harry stopped me.

"I wonder if he knows how to speak Japanese," Harry said.

"I don't know," I said. "That's one thing I didn't think to ask him."

"I guess he wouldn't have to," Harry said. "Because all those Japs speak English these days."

He used the word several times and wound up getting a letter of protest from the Japanese consulate, which didn't appreciate him saying the word and considered it derogatory.

They were intimating that Harry was a bigot or a racist. But Harry was nothing of the kind. He didn't care where a person was from or what they looked like. He made all of his decisions based on how a guy played baseball or what a person knew about the game.

But Harry's philosophy was always that the best defense is a good offense, and he never took anything lying down. He wrote a letter back to the consulate and let them know what he thought of their letter.

At the time there was a great bar owner in Chicago of Japanese descent who took the name "Tommy O'Leary" when he first got here, but everyone knew he was Japanese. So when Harry wrote the letter back to the consulate, he said, "I'm not racist and I'll prove it to you. I talked to my good friends Yosh Kawano and Tommy O'Leary and they said nothing's wrong with using that word."

Well, I could just see the guy at the Japanese consulate reading the letter thinking, "Tommy O'Leary? What does he know about it?"

In 1995, Harry got himself into trouble again. Prior to a game at Wrigley Field which was to feature the Dodgers' Japanese sensation Hideo Nomo, Harry—now eighty years old—referred to his own eyes as "slanty" on a radio show. Needless to say, his insensitive remark caused another huge outcry. But Harry's thoughts on such things were, "If a guy has slanty eyes, why can't I say he has slanty eyes? If he had brown eyes, I could say he has brown eyes, couldn't I?"

We're not here to debate political correctness, because there was no such thing with Harry. But if you were around him a lot, as I was, you knew he wasn't a racist. You should have heard how angry he was whenever he stumbled upon a country club that excluded one minority or another.

I knew Harry for twenty-five years, and I don't think racism ever played into anything he did. He said a lot of things that would have concerned me if they had come from someone else, but Harry just spoke without thinking much beforehand.

He didn't think first and he didn't care second. It's like the line he had about liking alleged wiseguy Tony Accardo. He liked him because he treated Harry nicely. He didn't care what else this guy might have done to others. Harry had a very simple, if not naive, way of looking at life. "I'll treat you how you treat me," was pretty much the extent of it.

Harry idolized Bob Gibson. He told me more than once that he thought of him as a god because of what he did for the St. Louis Cardinals. He didn't care if he was black, green, or blue. People thought at times that Harry had ulterior motives, but I never saw it. I never sensed it. I never believed it.

He told me a thousand times that Jackie Robinson was absolutely the most exciting player he'd ever seen. Ever. In fifty-three years in the game, there was no one he enjoyed watching more than Jackie Robinson.

All Harry knew was Jackie made the game fun, just like Ryne Sandberg and Sammy Sosa. He loved guys who could run and make things happen, and that was his criteria for liking a person. Maybe that was too simple, but that was Harry.

One night over cocktails, he told me what it was like in the '40s and '50s and '60s.

"Our radio station was picked up in all the southern states when I was in St. Louis," Harry said. "And I used to get letters from people all the time calling me racist names because I loved Jackie Robinson. They called me a 'you-know-what lover' because I thought he was a great player. Can you believe that crap? What makes people so damn sick?"

Harry wouldn't say the word. That's how much of a racist he was. He received death threats from lunatic bigots for saying Jackie Robinson was perhaps his favorite player ever at that time. That's how much of a racist he was. He endangered his own safety to stick up for a great player. That's how much of a racist Harry Caray was.

Buy Me Some Ham and Some Cracker Jacks

Controversy followed Harry Caray everywhere, from city to city and from ballpark to ballpark. And even on a day as seemingly harmless as "Cracker Jack" Celebration Day, Harry managed to cause a stir.

It was in 1993 at Wrigley Field when Cracker Jack celebrated its 100th anniversary, and "Jack" came out to the ballpark to let the fans in on the festivities. They had "Jack" dressed up and parading around in front of the park and hanging around on the field and giving away boxes of goodies to lucky fans.

Cubs marketing director John McDonough helped orchestrate the day and everything was going fabulously until I read some copy on the air about how Cracker Jack sponsored the day, gave away boxes, and yada, yada, yada. I thought it was absolutely the most innocent promotion, but Harry glared at me like I'd stolen his lunch money.

"Can you imagine a five-year-old kid, a little orphan kid, scraping together his pennies, enough money to buy Cracker Jacks?" Harry began. "And after eating the whole box and waiting breathlessly for the prize at the bottom, there's no prize on the bottom of the box?

"That's false advertising and there ought to be a Senate

investigation into Cracker Jack prizes. It's a terrible thing to break a young kid's heart like that."

Moments later, Arne superimposed the head of Cracker Jack on the body of PR assistant Chuck Wasserstrom. And that's when Harry went nuts—for real. Harry yelled, "They got to you too, Arne? Oh, no. Not you too, Arne. Are they paying you off, too?"

That went on for about another half-inning and apparently the Cracker Jacks people were so upset that they wanted to see a tape of it and looked into legal recourse. Poor John McDonough, the Cubs' marketing director, had to field a battery of calls from people who represented Cracker Jack until the Great Cracker Jack Controversy finally died down.

I just wonder if during the 20,000 or so times that he sang "Take Me Out to the Ball Game," did he ever stop to consider that he was saying, "buy me some peanuts and Cracker Jacks?"

Maybe it's a good thing I never mentioned that to him, or that could have been the end of a great tradition.

Speaking of tradition, every year around Christmas I'd get a ham from Harry. I was on the ham list like hundreds of his other friends, and it arrived every year as sure as the snow in Chicago. And every year I'd call Harry and thank him. Every December I'd also point out to him that being Jewish, I'm a little more partial to turkey than ham.

"Oh, great," Harry would say. "I'm glad you liked it."

"Merry Christmas, Harry," I'd say. "See you in a few weeks."

And the next year I'd be right back on the ham list again. I never had the heart to tell him, but Harry would've been happy to know was that I always gave it to the chef, Carlos, at one of our restaurants, and his family enjoyed it very much.

Among the many millions who mourned Harry's death was Carlos, who I'm sure was thinking about that ham when he heard the tragic news.

No one ate ham the night I had dinner with Harry and Barry Rozner at Don and Charley's, the famous restaurant in Scottsdale, and we were discussing the problems in the Middle East and whether there would ever be peace.

Out of nowhere, Harry says, "You know those Israelians are great fighters." Barry and I looked at each other and said, "Israelians?"

"Yeah," Harry said. "The Israelians. You know one thing I can't understand is why those Israelians and those Arabs can't get along. They all live in the same area for God's sakes. All there is over there is sand, so what the hell are they fighting over?"

Rozner was still choking on his steak, so I said, "Well, Harry, it's pretty much about religious difference and land and water and a couple of thousand years of fighting over territory and things like that. But I can't sit here in the next five minutes and explain it to you any more than I could the problems between the English and the Irish, who've been fighting for hundreds of years over religious and territorial differences."

"Well, I don't know about that," Harry said. "Maybe they ought to just make them play eighteen games every season and at the end of the year see who makes out on top."

Now, how can you argue with that?

Harry and I never argued about golf for the simple reason that he wouldn't play golf with me. When I first began broadcasting in Chicago I was looking for a golf partner for the road trips and in Chicago during the summers, so I asked Harry about his golf game.

"You know what, Steve," he chuckled, "I gave it up cold turkey thirty years ago. It was ruining my cheery disposition."

Harry decided, actually, that what most people do at country clubs is play golf in the morning, eat lunch, play cards all day, and drink all night. And Harry liked that program OK, except for the golf part. So for the benefit of his temperament, he skipped the golf and went right to the rest of the day.

Thing is, by the time I met him, his temperament in the morning was about the same as that of anyone having a lousy day on the golf course, so I guess he might just as well have continued to play.

There was another thing Harry didn't play: night baseball on the North Side of Chicago. Harry hated the idea of night baseball at Wrigley Field and until the day he died, he was sorry that they ever did it—even though he stopped talking about it publicly.

"I knew it would happen and I knew it had to happen because of TV," Harry said. "But I'm so afraid it will kill the popularity of Cubs baseball. I'm afraid it will kill the idea of walking to the park and the idea of kids taking the train with their families to the park.

"It's not like it used to be. Nobody walks the street at night or takes the train at night anymore, Steve. It's going to kill what they have going here. As sure as God made green apples, night baseball will kill the Cubs."

Harry didn't mind night games as much as long as there were women around, and there were always plenty of women around. But it was very rare that I would bring a woman into the booth because I didn't want my date to become a part of the broadcast.

Harry—who loved women of all races, sizes, shapes, and nationalities—always kissed the hand or cheek or lips of every woman who ever entered the booth, including Hillary Clinton.

On one occasion, I brought a date up to the booth and Harry got up to greet her. One of his famous sayings when he saw a younger woman was, "Young lady, you need an older man in your life." He said that every time he saw me with a date. But this young lady turned the tables on him.

She looked at me, looked back at Harry, and said, "Harry, I have no need for another older man, I already have one." And she pointed right at me as Harry fell back in his chair laughing. That was one of the few times I ever saw Harry speechless.

Harry was married three times and he told unbelievably funny stories about what it was like paying alimony all those years.

His most famous one, however, involved an anniversary.

"I've been married three times, and I've probably paid alimony longer than anyone in history," Harry was known to say. "My first marriage fell apart because it was my fault, the second one was her fault, and the third one is perfect.

"My first wife was a wonderful woman. It was all my fault that we didn't stay together. But in 1979 I was sending her checks and thinking, 'Holy Cow, I've been doing this for thirty years already. How long will this go on?' So I put that in a note with my monthly check.

"Two days later I got a letter back that said: 'Dearest Harry, till death do us part.'"

Limos, Boats, and All Those Meals

In his later years, Harry had a special routine in New York City. He would stay at the Regency Hotel and walk to various restaurants and bars near the hotel after the game.

One familiar haunt was The Copa. And every time Harry arrived, there was a guy sitting at a back table with his back to the wall in the back of the establishment. Over the course of a few years, Harry began to wave to the guy since they sort of knew each other by sight, and eventually the guy started sending Harry a drink each time he came in. Harry would, in turn, send one back, and this went on for years.

But one time, around 6:30 in the evening, Harry said to the bartender, "You know, I've been trading drinks with that guy for years and years, and I've never even met him. But he looks familiar. Who is that guy?"

"You don't know who that is?" asked the bartender. "You've got to be joking."

"Listen, pal," Harry replied, "if I knew who he was, I wouldn't be asking you."

"Well, Harry," the bartender said sheepishly, "that's Frank Costello."

"You mean Frank Costello, the mob boss of New York?" Harry asked. "You're kidding."

"Listen, pal," the bartender said, giving Harry a taste of his own medicine, "if I was kidding, that's not something I would kid about."

So Harry got up from his chair and took a stroll back to see Frank Costello.

"Hey, Frank," Harry said, shaking his hand. "For years we've been waving to each other and buying each other drinks, and I had no idea who you were until tonight."

"Harry," Costello said, "that's the difference between your business and my business. Before I took a sip of the first drink you sent me, I made sure I knew who you were."

But Harry didn't mind at all. Harry told me many times that he knew Tony "the Big Tuna" Accardo for years and thought he was a terrific fellow, too.

"He's not a bad guy at all," Harry said. "I ran into him Palm Springs a few times and he was very nice to me. I never asked him about his business and he never asked me about mine. We got along fine."

New York always meant a grand time for Harry, because a town that never sleeps was built for the man who could go without a snooze for months at a time. He was the exact opposite of a bear, which must sleep for months at a time during the winter. Harry could stay awake for an entire winter, making up for some of the accidental rest he got during the summer while broadcasting.

And whenever Harry was in New York he'd hook up with his old pal Mickey Mantle, one of the few humans who could go toe-to-toe with Harry for an evening and match him drink for drink. And Mantle was also one of the few guys Harry envied, because he had a lifestyle Harry could really appreciate.

He also loved Mickey Mantle the player. On more than one

occasion, Harry told me he felt Mickey Mantle could have been the greatest baseball player of all time.

"I'm not saying he was, Steve, because he wasn't," Harry said. "But if he hadn't gotten hurt, I think he would have been. There was nothing he couldn't do on a baseball field. Nothing. It's kind of a waste of talent that he wasn't the greatest ever, but he's up near the top and he had a great career. And Mickey doesn't apologize for it, either, because he says he had fun doing it."

Fun was never lacking when Harry and Mickey got together, and one winter evening they encouraged broadcaster Don Drysdale—another of Harry's favorites when he pitched—to join them when the three found themselves together at a banquet.

"Steve, you know I did some silly things over the years but I never thought I'd do something this stupid," Harry said, shaking his head. "But it got to be about 3 A.M. and Mickey says, 'Fellas, let's go to Atlantic City.' I said, 'Fine with me.' And Don agreed. But Mickey then proceeds to tell us that he can't get a car. 'That's ridiculous,' I said. 'I can get us a car in five minutes.'

"Mickey says, 'No need to. I've got our transportation out front.' And when we get outside, there's three girls in bikinis on motorcycles. Don sees this and says, 'Gentlemen, I'm done for the night.' And he runs over and grabs a cab and that was it for him.

"That was my first instinct, too, but I decided I had to find out what this was all about. Now, it's about 20 degrees out and the wind is blowing hard so I can't imagine what those girls must have felt like, because I was freezing my behind off. But I played along with the joke and was starting to get worried when we got to the top of one of the bridges—I couldn't even tell you which one—and everyone gets off the bikes and into a limo.

"I said, 'Mickey, I wasn't going to be the one to say uncle

first, but am I glad you didn't take us all the way there on those bikes because I was starting to believe it.' And Mick says, 'Harry, I just wanted to put a little excitement in your life. Now, sit back and relax and enjoy the ride.'

"And we did. But I'll never forget the five minutes I spent on that motorbike, Steve. That was Mickey. He just wanted to have a little fun and entertain his friends. He was a lot of fun to be around and I really miss him."

Going out to dinner with Harry was always an interesting experience, even without the motorcycles. And I recall a night in Houston in the late '80s when Harry dragged along famous Chicago baseball columnist Jerome Holtzman. It was after the game and already past midnight when we all set off for a "snack."

"Hey, Harry," Jerome began joyfully, "I've got a real taste for Chinese food. C'mon, I'll pay for it."

"Well," Harry answered, "first of all, we're getting Italian food because that's what I eat every night after the game. That's what I eat about 360 nights a year and I'm not changing tonight. And secondly, I'm paying for it. And if you don't like any of that, then you better get out of the limo right now and go back to the hotel because that's the way it is."

And that's the way it was. Jerry, naturally, agreed with whatever Harry wanted, because whatever Harry wanted is exactly what Harry got.

One thing you may not know about Harry's dining habits is that he never allowed menus to be brought to the table until he and his guests were sipping their fourth martini. That was the rule, and that's the way it was. Well, when you were eating after a game, it might be 12:30 or 1 o'clock in the morning before you actually sat down, but that didn't stop Harry's pre-dinner ritual.

One night in Pittsburgh, Harry called ahead to one of his favorite places, Tambolini's on the Hill. Harry often called ahead to a place he knew well and had them stay open especially for him. These restaurants or bars were always happy to do it, because it meant good business, a good time, and lots of free publicity. But on this one night in Pittsburgh, Tambolini's would've been closed already had Harry not called ahead. So the owner kept the kitchen staff and waiters and waitresses—and especially the bartender—around for Harry.

But as martini piled on top of martini, the owner stopped me as I headed for the rest room.

"Steve," he begged, "can't you get him to please look at the menu?"

"My good man," I replied. "How long have you known Harry?"

"Oh, years," he said. "Many years."

"Well then, have you ever known him to open a menu before his fourth drink?" I asked.

"No," he said, lowering his head. "No, he never has."

"Then, there's your answer," I chuckled. "All you can do is what we all do, make the best of it and have some drinks and laughs along the way."

So the entire staff stuck around while Harry had his four martinis, his salad, his Budweisers, his veal chop with lingui-ni and clam sauce, and his Grand Marnier afterward. And by the time we left at about 3 A.M., everyone was happy except the poor guy who had to clean up and the owner who had to lock up. And there's about a thousand restaurant and bar owners throughout baseball who could tell you the same story.

To say that Harry usually stayed out late is an understatement. One morning, fellow broadcaster Don Drysdale noticed Harry had a particularly tough evening (and morning) when he saw Harry's puffy eyes through those thick glasses. As they boarded a plane and headed off for the next city, Don stopped him in his tracks.

"Harry," said Don, "you look like a bullfrog looking through a keg of ice."

One thing about Harry that always looked perfect was his wild and wavy white hair. He used to get it cut once a week, making him the only man this side of Bill Clinton to visit a barber that often.

When he was in Arizona for spring training, he'd drive over to the Phoenician Hotel every Thursday and see Stan Demory, who was known in Scottsdale as the "barber to the stars." And every Thursday he'd tell Stan that he wanted it to look a special way.

"Stan, I want it to look like Bob's Big Boy," Harry would say. "Flop it up real nice on top so it looks like Bob's Big Boy."

Considering all the fancy and expensive restaurants Harry ate at during his life, it seems a tad ironic that he modeled his looks after Bob's Big Boy. But then again, Harry's middle name was "contradiction," so actually it makes perfect sense to me.

Being in Harry's limo always meant some interesting conversation, especially on get-away night. Harry would usually invite Arne Harris and me to ride along with him. As we headed for the airport, the only thing on Harry's mind was an airport hotel and a couple of drinks.

We were usually about an hour ahead of the team, so that

gave Harry a chance to load up before the flight. We'd have three or four or five drinks and then drive over to the tarmac and wait for the team bus to board the plane.

Well, on one evening in 1993, the bus was there but the plane wasn't, so we sat in the limo and began another conversation about the Cubs' pitching staff, and that's when Harry spotted Ron Santo standing outside the car.

"Ron, get in here," Harry bellowed. "I want to ask you something."

I kicked Arne's shoe and whispered, "This is going to be good."

"What's up, Harry?" Ron asked, not realizing Harry was already tipsy and in an argumentative mood.

"Hey, where's all the goddamn pitching you always talk about?" Harry yelled.

A stunned Santo wasn't sure what to say. Ron, who was a great, great player and will someday be in the Hall of Fame, also happens to be the biggest Cub fan in the world. He probably cares more about the team than anyone, and he believed the team had some good, young pitching on the way.

"Well, where the hell is it?" Harry asked again. "All I hear you talk about is our great young pitching and I don't see any of it. We can't get anybody out and I don't see anyone coming up here who can get anyone out."

"Well, Harry," Ron began, trying to defend himself, "they're just kids, like twenty years old. You can't just bring them up without experience. I saw some of them in spring training and . . ."

"Well, if they're so goddamned good, then get them up here already!" Harry said. "Where are you going to get better experience than here in the big leagues? I don't know where you get your facts, but I don't think you know what you're talking about. I'm tired of hearing about all the great young arms. I don't think there are any. If we had them, they'd be up here already."

This went on for about twenty minutes. I can't say I felt bad for Ron because I had been on the receiving end of that so many times that I was just glad it wasn't me. I kept kicking Arne and laughing under my breath, but I didn't want Harry to look at me. When Harry was on the warpath, it was like being called on in class when you didn't study the night before. It could be terrifying.

Harry didn't go out with players very much because he liked a big dinner before he hit the streets, and the players were much more likely to eat the free spread in the clubhouse and get right out to the bars. They also had to get in earlier because they had to play the next day, while Harry expected to come to the park feeling the effects of the evening's activities. On some days I believe he even thrived on it.

That doesn't mean he wouldn't bump into a few of the players from time to time, but as the separation between media and players—church and state, if you will—became more exaggerated in Harry's later years, it was less likely that they'd be running into each other at the same spots. I think the game in general saw a much closer relationship between the players, broadcasters, and writers when they all rode on trains together and spent so much more time together. That was also long before the days of Watergate and investigative journalism, which has become a big part of sports, too.

So the last twenty years of Harry's broadcasting career, he spent most of his evenings with friends and broadcasters and acquaintances. He also didn't mind being alone when he began the evening, because it never stayed that way very long. Harry Caray was every fan's friend, and whatever establishment he walked into became one big party room for as long as he decided to stay there. Harry also liked to dine with managers, coaches, and executives, but always with the understanding that if they weren't ready to go when he was, they'd have to find their own transportation to the restaurant.

I'll never forget the night in 1990 when Harry was supposed to take Cubs manager Don Zimmer out to dinner in Montreal, but Zimmer, understandably, couldn't be ready to go fifteen minutes after the game was over, and that's when Harry wanted to leave. Well, Harry got so impatient waiting for Zimmer that he finally told his limo driver to leave Olympic Stadium.

The limo brought Harry to the restaurant and Harry sent it back to get Zimmer, who was so mad that he refused to get into the car and just took the bus back to the hotel.

Apparently, this wasn't the first time it happened to Zim, but it was the last time he ever made plans with Harry for a night out after the game.

Pete Vonachen's brilliantly funny eulogy made clear several things about Harry, not the least of which was his terrible backseat driving. But while Harry criticized Pete for being a horrendous driver, there may have been no worse driver on this planet or any other than Harry himself.

During one bad day in 1986 I had the misfortune of being his passenger when I met him at his Scottsdale hotel and he insisted that he drive us to dinner that night.

Well, Harry was color blind, and I don't think I have to tell you that the stoplights have color in them and that it's difficult to see what position those lights are in at night when you're flying through an intersection.

I already knew he was color blind from the way he used to dress himself, but this night gave me an even more horrifying sight. Every time we went through an intersection, Harry would drop down from the posted speed limit of 45 mph to about 5 mph, causing the cars behind us to come screeching to a halt. We did this stopping and starting thing all the way to

Tomasso's with cars swerving around us and in front of us all the way there.

And once we got there, Harry had his four martinis and his three or four Budweisers and then his Grand Marniers afterward. Of course, he then insisted on driving us back to his hotel and we went through the same road test on the return voyage, coming within a hair of several major collisions and chain-reaction disasters.

And when I got out of the car, after he scared ten years off of my life, I got down and kissed the ground, and I pledged never to set foot in an automobile again if he was behind the wheel.

And I never did.

Harry's good friend, "the prominent Chicago attorney, Jack Barry," has a home in the Lake Geneva area of Wisconsin, and Harry almost always traveled up there for the All-Star break. Whenever I could, I'd meet Harry up at Jack's house for at least an afternoon or evening of fun, as Jack always invited many of his friends to take part in the festivities.

Jack had a boat on the lake and we usually took a spin or two around which was always a riot, since Harry was frequently several Buds ahead of the pack by the time we all got on the boat. On one particular day, we went out for a ride, but the boat stopped working right in the middle of the lake—just stopped dead in the water. Jack figured out that one of the lines had gotten caught in the propeller, and that's what was holding things up.

Well, Jack looked at me, I looked at Harry, and Harry looked at Jack. Clearly none of the three of us was capable or willing to do anything about it, so we all turned to Pete Vonachen, the only other human being aboard the yacht. So sure enough, Pete looked at the three of us, shook his head, and jumped overboard. He submerged himself completely and did his best Lloyd Bridges imitation while untangling the rope from the blades.

He looked like a bloated rainbow trout when he finally got back up on board, where the rest of us were sipping our beers and having a nice time. Pete looked at the frivolity and said, "Harry, for Christ's sake, couldn't you have helped me a little bit?"

Harry just giggled that great giggle, which made you laugh in and of itself, and said, "Pete, the only thing I could've done was drown myself and probably blow up the boat. Next thing you know, you'll want me to drive the damn boat around the lake."

"No!" Pete screamed. "Forget it. Forget I said anything. No driving, definitely no driving."

Harry loved baseball so much that he could never get enough of it, no matter what the situation. I recall a very long night in Pittsburgh. We had rain delays and extra innings and got out of Three Rivers Stadium at about 2 A.M.

This was in the days before Harry had a limo, so we grabbed a cab to head back to the hotel. Harry jumped in front and I got in the back with Arne, and you could plainly see that this cabby had little more in his car than a walkie-talkie and a meter. But Harry wanted to hear a baseball game on the radio.

"Hey, buddy, can you get the White Sox game on that?" Harry asked.

"No, sir," he said. "I have no radio."

"Well, how about the Giants and Dodgers?" Harry said. "I know they're still playing."

"But I don't have a radio," the cabby repeated.

"Well, do you know the score of the White Sox game? Can you get that on that thing?" Harry asked.

"No, sir," the cabby answered. "I don't think you understand. I can only call the base with this radio."

"Well, Christ," Harry responded. "I don't understand what kind of damn radio that can be if you can't get a score of a ball game on it."

And the cabby just shook his head, trying not to make it any worse. But that was Harry. He just did four hours of baseball and two hours of rain delays and he still wanted to hear more about baseball.

Back when he was really pitching the beer big time, the surest way to get mentioned by Harry on the broadcast was to send up a note saying you were a "Bud Man and a Cub Fan." That was automatic.

The absolutely certain way to ensure not getting on the air was to send up money. Harry was nothing if not consistent with that. A lot of people thought he mentioned restaurants or bars so that he could eat free or drink free, but that was never the case. He paid his own way. Period.

"If you want to buy me a drink, that's fine," Harry would say. "If I like this place, I'll mention it on the air but only because I like it. If you pay for my dinner, I'll never mention it again."

The free plugs he gave were his way of helping someone, because the guy dearest to his heart was the bartender. It wasn't a free plug because he wanted the undying gratitude of saloon keepers and restaurant owners. He did it because he knew those people worked hard for a living. He spent a good portion of his life with them and he was very gracious with his plugs, as anyone who ever listened knows. But he never took anything for it.

I'll bet you didn't know that.

◆❖◆

Harry ate big meals every night, usually in the middle of the night, but he never exercised—at least not the way most people exercise. While other people would work out physically, Harry disdained physical exercise. Harry got his blood flowing by arguing, and I believe that kept him alive for about an extra twenty-five years.

Most people use a treadmill or play racquetball or walk eighteen holes or lift weights, but Harry felt the best exercise was fighting with words. And while most of us strive for inner peace, look for ways to calm ourselves, and hope for tranquility on a daily basis, Harry despised calm. That was the antithesis of Harry.

Even if a subject was totally unrelated to what was happening on the field, it didn't matter. It also didn't matter what the argument was about or what side I was on. Harry would take the other side and debate you into the ground. The thing that aggravated him the most was when he was ready to argue and you didn't respond. He'd get mad and make another statement even more outrageous than the first one in hopes that eventually you'd have to venture an opinion.

Then, you had a brawl of verbal blows that you can't imagine, and that happened every day of my life with Harry.

Even with Harry gone, I still find myself on the way to the yard every day preparing for an argument. It may take me years to get over that adrenaline rush—not to mention the fear.

The Harry Chronicles

always felt like Bill Veeck and Harry Caray were made for one another. It certainly was a great time in baseball when they became owner and announcer together on the South Side of Chicago.

There's no doubt that Bill was the greatest innovator the game has ever known and having played for him, I can tell you that he might have been the smartest man I've ever met. If he's not, he's in the top two or three.

Bill was a great salesman and always had an eye out for the fans. If you were able to pick one owner over the course of baseball history who really had the fans' best interests at heart when he did something, it was Bill Veeck.

His counterpart in the broadcast booth was Harry Caray, who also cared more about the fans than anything else in his life. People will tell you about the legendary beer consumption of Bill Veeck and the legendary consumption of anything alcoholic by Harry, and you would think that they must have had a lot of great nights out together during their years with the White Sox.

But that wasn't true at all.

"You know, Steve," Harry once told me, "it hurt my feelings that Bill never invited me out and always turned me down when I asked him to go out. For years it bothered me and finally one day I asked him about it.

"He said, 'Harry, it would be the easiest thing in the world for you and I to go drinking together, but we're trying to sell the White Sox to the City of Chicago. We're trying to sell tickets, and we can double the coverage if you go to your places and I go to mine and we find a few new places every night. I know that's what you do and that's certainly what I do, so look at all the people we're meeting with and talking White Sox baseball. If we go out together, we're wasting time. This way we can be in two places at one time.'

"And you know what, Steve, he was exactly right."

Harry had the utmost respect for Bill Veeck and felt like we all did about spending time with Bill. When you were with Bill, you were in the presence of greatness. You understood that a showman of his like would never again be seen in baseball. I have a feeling Bill felt the same way about Harry. They were absolute originals and two of the most intelligent and entertaining people you could ever want to meet.

From my standpoint, I was very fortunate that I got a chance to play for one of them and broadcast next to the other, and that added up to many of the greatest experiences of my life. I considered it an honor to be able to walk up the stairs at Comiskey Park and find Bill, and just talk with him about the world around us. Sometimes it involved baseball, but usually not. He was so well read and so interesting to talk to.

And though Harry didn't read books the way Bill did, Harry was a voracious reader of newspapers and magazines and there was nothing happening in the world that he didn't know about.

Looking back on it now, I consider it a privilege to have known them both.

I think two of Harry's favorite players were Stan Musial and Ryne Sandberg. Whenever he talked about the greatest players he ever saw, those were always the first two names he mentioned. Of course, Harry loved to promote his own players, and was also very fond of Andre Dawson, Rick Sutcliffe, Mark Grace, and Sammy Sosa.

Off the field, I think his favorite player had to be Mickey Mantle, because Harry would go drinking with him in New York and Mickey was one of the few guys on the planet capable of going with Harry for an entire evening—not to mention morning.

I remember when the great George Brett made plans with Harry to meet up in Palm Springs one winter, because he wanted to get in on Harry's act. Even though Brett was forty-some years younger than Harry, he figured he'd spend about a week out there partying with Harry and getting the lay of the land.

Brett said he lasted about two days and had to call it quits. "I feared for my life," Brett said. "Harry was just too much."

As he proved time and time again, even younger, healthier, and stronger men couldn't keep up with Harry at night.

Harry was often too much for some White Sox players during his time on the South Side, where he was very critical of players like Carlos May, Rick Reichardt, and Bill Melton. That was in the vintage Harry Caray era that led into the Jimmy Piersall days when Harry was playing to a much different audience than he did in his run as the Cub Kahuna.

Harry began his career with the Cardinals (1945–69), and spent one year with Oakland (1970) before moving on to the White Sox (1971–81) and Cubs (1982–97).

But Harry said it was probably on the South Side that his true expressions of sadness or happiness began to come through like never before. If there was one out and a man on third and a guy popped out, Harry would scream, "He pahhh-huuuupped it up!" with a real disgusted voice.

The White Sox had a blue collar, South Side fandom that liked to hear him tell it like it was and Harry let fly with both barrels on the players. He was also on very small radio and television outlets, so he never had to worry about whom he might be offending, not that Harry ever thought much about that.

One of Harry's true favorites was Ben Stein, his longtime friend and business partner who passed away a few years before Harry died.

When he still attended games, Harry would always say, "Arne, get a shot of Ben Stein's seats and see if Ben's sitting down there today."

That was always good for a free plug, since Ben owned Harry Caray's Restaurant in Chicago, of which Harry got a piece of the action. Ben and Harry were legendary for their long and outrageous evenings together.

Harry loved to tell the story about how Ben went to one of those "World's Largest Office Party" nights at the Hyatt Regency in downtown Chicago, and bought a drink for the house. That ran him about $10,000, which Harry claimed had to be the costliest round ever bought.

Harry loved Ben, but when Ben got sick and was hospitalized, Harry insisted on having Arne get a shot of Thorek Hospital, which was right around the corner from Wrigley Field on Irving Park Road. Since he couldn't shoot Ben's seats, he wanted to see a picture of the hospital. And he asked for it over and over and over again, as if Ben might be waiting on the roof for Arne to get a shot of him.

"My good friend Ben Stein is watching the game over at Thorek Hospital," Harry would say. "Hey, Arne, get a shot of the hospital, would ya?"

Arne would do it and then get in my earpiece and say, "Would you get him off the hospital already?"

But that's what Harry wanted. The only thing is, if Ben was

watching the games as much as Harry said, there couldn't have been any time for rehab. But in any case, everyone tuned in to WGN was able to monitor Ben's progress on a daily basis.

Chef Abraham was another character who got a lot of air time, because he was the fabulous chef at Harry's restaurant. He's still there today and still makes the best chicken vesuvio I've ever had anywhere. My favorite meal there is a St. Louis specialty, the fried meat ravioli. But everything in the house pretty much comes down to the tender loving care of Chef Abraham.

Abraham had a few brothers. They're all very large men and all look exactly alike. You couldn't mistake them, but whenever they'd come to a game together and sit in the seats, Harry would point out Abraham and I'd say, "Harry, who do you think that is with him?"

"Oh, well, let's take another look, Arne," Harry would say. "Well, those must be Chef Abraham's brothers, and of course, Chef Abraham is the great chef and good friend of mine down at Harry Caray's Restaurant." Harry never missed an opportunity to plug.

I remember one day a reporter wrote a complimentary article about the restaurant, and Harry read the entire article on the air. It must have taken two innings. We missed three homers, a double, and a hit by pitch while he read word for word the article about every dish and piece of memorabilia in the joint.

"What's he doing?" Arne asked in my ear. "Is he going to read the entire thing?"

"It appears that way," I whispered to Arne. "There's no stopping him now."

Harry had no problem doing that. The idea of self-promotion was second nature.

◆❖◆

But while we kidded him about such things, you have to understand that Harry was also creating characters the way sitcoms create personalities. *Seinfeld* had Kramer, George, Elaine, Newman, and, of course, Jerry himself as master of his domain.

Harry ran the show—like Jerry—and had a cast of characters, which included myself and Arne and Ben Stein and Chef Abraham and the guys catching home run balls out on the street and Mandy Cohen and Joe Cornejo and Pete Vonachen and on and on and on.

Some people had recurring parts and some weren't asked back. Some went on to bigger and better things, and some had silent parts or were never seen. Arne was the great unseen character, like Carlton the Doorman in *Rhoda*. But at least you heard Carlton. Arne was the voice that you never heard and never saw (unless Harry's earpiece was hanging near my mike. Then, you heard Arne quite well).

But Harry made sure Arne was a big part of the broadcast. Harry was always holding one-way conversations, leaving the viewer completely confused. At times you'd hear Harry responding to Arne with yes or no answers to questions that you never heard at home.

Or even better, he'd have an entire conversation with Arne, giving only half the story. "You're kidding," Harry would say. "Arne, I had no idea. . . . Can we get that? . . . I hope it's not serious. . . ." And if you were at home, you just scratched your head. Harry created a family broadcast and a friendly atmosphere that transcended the Cubs and often overshadowed the team.

In most years, that wasn't hard to do.

What Arne did for Harry in return—and this is where Arne is brilliant—was make available to Harry all of the great shots that would help keep Harry interested and keep him selling the team and the game and the city. All of that was good for the team and the game and the city, not to mention Arne and WGN-TV. And Harry had so much fun that he never really understood the scope of it.

Arne has a great sense of when to cut to shots outside of the game itself, and bring in the cast of characters and the greatest set in television land today: Wrigley Field.

The stands at Wrigley Field are a story unto themselves, because it's not just a game taking place, but rather a three-hour afternoon adventure at the playground along the lake.

"Steve, baseball is the little kid eating a hot dog with his mom and dad, getting mustard all over his face," Harry told me early in the 1983 season. "It's the little old lady waving to the camera and hoping she's on TV. It's the sun and the cotton candy and the beer and the bleachers. That's baseball every bit as much as the game and I always feel like it's our job to let people at home feel that."

Arne knows just when to cut to the kids with the parents and then when to cut back to them again. If he finds a story that he thinks is appealing, he'll go back to it four or five times throughout the course of the game as the storyline continually changes and develops.

If someone was having a tough time getting the top off a box of popcorn, Arne would stay with it until we had a conclusion to the event. Arne would find a guy having trouble seeing through his binoculars, and kept the cameraman focused on him and cutting back until the guy figured out that he never took the lens caps off. And that gave Harry a chance to talk about something other than baseball, especially if the baseball game was nothing to write home about.

The funny part is Harry always wanted to know who the people were.

"Hey, Arne," he'd yell. "Who is that guy with the green hat right there?"

Arne would say, "How the hell do I know, Harry?"

He must have asked that question 100,000 times, and Arne rarely had the answer.

And they had their routines that they went to whenever it was appropriate. If, for example, it was a terribly long and tedious game, Arne would shoot a guy with a long, white beard, and say in Harry's ear for only him to hear, "How long have we been playing this game, Harry?"

Just then the shot of the guy with the white beard would come on the screen and on cue Harry would say, "I'll tell you how long this game's gone today, ladies and gentlemen: That guy was clean-shaven when the game began."

And Arne would shoot a group of nuns and say in Harry's ear, "Harry, watching the Cubs . . ."

"I know, Arne, I know, Arne," Harry would say with mock disdain, "watching the Cubs is getting to be a habit."

The WGN cameramen, who are the best in the business, would always shoot their quota of very nice looking women, especially when it was warm out and they were wearing less and less clothing. That led to some very funny moments, and I think that's what set Arne and the WGN telecasts apart from the rest of them.

On a daily basis, like a soap opera, it was the continuing saga of the Cubs and their fans at Wrigley Field. When the team wasn't very good, we had to do the other things to keep people interested and Arne and Harry had a good idea of how to keep it interesting.

Every time Arne would get a shot of a son or daughter riding on daddy's shoulders, Harry would say, "There's the best seat in the house right there." And that made everyone feel good and that made people want to tune in the next day or come to the park in person.

They got pictures of very young fans or very old fans and sometimes three or four generations of fans all in the same family, sitting together in the brilliant sunshine at Wrigley Field.

And Harry knew exactly what to say and exactly what Arne was thinking. Those might have been Harry's trademarks, but they were set up by Arne. It was a team effort, but Arne was the master choreographer.

One way Harry would get Arne involved early in the season was with shoes—white shoes to be exact. That was a big thing with Arne, because he would never wear white shoes until Memorial Day, and then he'd wear them every day until Labor Day. Harry loved that, so he'd ask about the shoes every day leading up to Memorial Day and then make a big deal out of it until the day finally arrived.

Harry was very generous as far as Arne and I were concerned. Almost without exception, Harry would pay for everything whenever we went out for dinner and drinks. On the air, he used to talk about how I never picked up a check. Well, that was true, but that's because he wouldn't let me. But he'd get on me and then I'd get on Arne and we all had some yucks.

Then, one night in San Diego the stadium was invaded by millions of moths, though I have no idea why. They were everywhere around Jack Murphy Stadium and that set Harry off for about half an inning and he insisted on knowing where the moths were coming from.

They were dive-bombing the booth and bouncing all around and we were swatting with everything we had in us to get them away from our faces. They were all over the lights and in front of the cameras. It was like one of the plagues had set in on us.

"Hey, Harry," I said, "I don't want to cast any aspersions on your character or anything, but last inning, you went into your wallet to get something and now this inning, all of a sudden, there are moths all over the place. I don't know if there's any correlation, but we've been inundated with moths ever since you took your wallet out."

"Boy, oh boy," Harry said, staring at me with humorous contempt. "You've got a lot of nerve. When was the last time you picked up a check?"

And on and on he went for about two innings, but it gave us a chance to goof around and get Arne involved and he could brag about his generosity and rip me and Arne for being stingy at the same time.

Whenever Harry began an on-air discussion with, "You know, Steve, you're a college-educated guy," I knew I was in trouble. That meant he had recently discovered something that had nothing to do with the game and probably nothing to do with anything I had any prior knowledge of.

So on a day in 1996, Harry hit me with that phrase and then said, "So explain to me what this means. I'm driving home yesterday and I see this sign for seedless grapes. That's right, seedless grapes. Can you imagine that?

"I've never seen that. I've always loved grapes but I had to stop eating them years ago because I hated spitting out the seeds all the time. So here I was, face to face with a seedless grape and I had my driver pull over and I got some seedless grapes and they were fabulous. It was a great day. Can you imagine? Seedless grapes. What a thing.

"So here's my question to you, Steve: Where in the heck did they get seedless grapes? How can they do that?"

Well, I didn't have the heart to tell Harry that seedless grapes had been around for about fifteen years, so I said, "Not being a grapeologist and not being a genius in that field, I imagine that they're some sort of a hybrid, Harry. It's probably some kind of genetic engineering where they go into the lab and cross a number of types of grapes until they get the seedless variety."

"Well, that sounds pretty good," Harry said. "But how do I know if it's true?"

"I don't know," I said. "It did sound pretty good. I kind of surprised myself there, but I don't know if it's right."

So this went on for the better part of an inning-and-a-half as we discussed Harry's amazing grape discovery, and finally Arne got a call in the truck from a guy named Dave Thomas. Not the Wendy's guy, but he was apparently from the Napa Valley and very familiar with the great grape story. He said that my explanation was essentially right.

So Arne told us through our earpieces and Harry was ecstatic. Now he not only knew that seedless grapes existed but he knew how they were created.

"Geez, what a great day this is," Harry exclaimed. "I'm so happy about this grape thing. Now if only they could come up with a seedless watermelon because I really hate those seeds."

I know what you're thinking, but we only had an inning left to play so I didn't say a word.

Arne didn't think it was good idea to get real political on the air, so he always warned Harry when we were going to have a politician in the booth.

One day the mayor of Chicago, Richard M. Daley, was going

to visit with us for a few minutes and discuss a program he was putting in place that would involve baseball and the youth of Chicago. Arne suggested to Harry that since it was an election year, we keep the conversation away from politics.

So, naturally, Harry continued the tradition of listening to about a third of what Arne told him and said, "Hey, Mr. Mayor, I'm so glad you could be here. I know Arne Harris is very happy you're here because he announced to me a few minutes ago that he was going to vote for you for mayor this year!"

Now, the fact that Arne lives outside the city and can't vote, or that he said nothing of the kind, didn't enter into it all. Harry just wanted to say it and get a laugh at Arne's expense, so he did.

Harry was just as fascinating a person off the air as he was on, and one example was the way he felt about politics. He never mentioned much whether he liked the Democrats or Republicans. I believe he was registered, but I don't know which party he regularly voted for. One thing he said often was that he liked the individual more than the political affiliation.

He walked around for years with "Ross Perot" stickers on his suitcase and could be heard singing his praises until the day he died.

He also loved Rush Limbaugh, but not because of what he said necessarily. I think he liked the way he said it and the way he entertained people. It struck a strong cord with Harry. I know he went to see the show at least once when we were in New York. He was fascinated by Rush and always tried to get to see him when we hit the Big Apple.

Harry loved television, plain and simple. He loved TV. In fact, his wife, Dutchie, said one of the most disturbing things about seeing him unconscious in a hospital room before he died was that when she walked into the room, the TV wasn't turned on.

"It was very strange," she said. "You know with Harry, the TV was always on."

And when it came to the big events, Harry was glued to the set. There was no greater example of that than the O.J. Simpson trial.

If you wanted to know anything about the O.J. trial, all you had to do was ask Harry. He must have worn out a picture tube during that escapade because he didn't miss an hour. He'd come to the park every day and he would be livid about something Johnnie Cochran did or something F. Lee Bailey tried to get away with.

Day after day after day for the entire length of the Simpson trial, Harry watched nearly every minute, and I'm sure Dutchie never wants to hear the words "O.J. Simpson trial" ever again.

But if you ever need to know anything about it, just ask me, because Harry recited every word of it to me, and it's one of those things you just never forget.

Harry's view of politics often centered on how an issue or an election would affect him, and therefore I'm certain he would have taken a very pragmatic view of Bill Clinton's scandal involving Monica Lewinsky in 1998.

"I don't understand," Harry would have said. "I mean, why in the world are they making such a big deal out of it? My Budweiser stock and my Tribune stock are doing very well, so what's the problem? I'll tell you this much: I'm going to be pretty goddamn pissed off if they sink the economy because of this. The economy was just fine before they decided to find out what was going on in the White House.

"All I know is I got a call from Ronald Reagan and I can't

remember ever getting a call from Bill Clinton. I kissed his wife once, so maybe he's mad at me."

Many people had many different opinions about Harry, but there are some things I'm certain of.

For example, I agreed with Arne Harris when he said there'll never be another broadcaster who becomes a bigger star than the players themselves.

"You'll never again see a guy bigger than the team or the sport he broadcasts," Arne said. "It'll never happen again. Harry is bigger than the game of baseball and bigger than the Cubs. He's an icon."

Former partner Jimmy Piersall, now a Cubs minor league coach, says Harry was more than just the greatest broadcaster ever.

"Harry made the game fun for the fans and he never considered himself bigger than the average fan," Piersall said. "He's the voice of the common man. He's a guy sitting in his living room having a beer and enjoying the game. That's why people loved him so much, and boy did the people love him. He was worth about a million tickets a year to the Cubs, and they'll never have another guy like that. It's impossible, because Harry was a once-in-a-lifetime guy."

CHAPTER
14

Of Mice and Milo

Back in 1980, new Cubs broadcaster Milo Hamilton had been promised the No. 1 job when Jack Brickhouse retired. And as the summer breezes of 1981 turned into the cold winds of September, there was a sort of ceremonial passing of the microphone from the legendary Brickhouse to Hamilton.

And on the final day of the season, there was much sadness and celebration in the booth, as Brickhouse—an immensely popular figure in the Midwest—ended his Hall of Fame career, and gave up his seat to Hamilton. Milo had joined the broadcast crew only two years earlier with the expectation that he would one day take over controls of the ship.

But a funny thing happened on the way to the throne. During the strike-shortened season of 1981, the Wrigley family sold the Cubs to the Tribune Company.

Harry—then with the White Sox—was never one to miss out on an opportunity, so he immediately called Andy McKenna, who was the Cubs' Chairman of the Board.

"Hey, Andy," Harry chuckled into the phone, "I'm surprised at you. I'm surprised that you haven't offered me the Cubs job."

"But, Harry," Andy pleaded, "you have a job."

"I do right now," Harry said, "but at the end of this season, I'll be a free agent and there isn't anyone better-suited to do Cubs games than me." And he was right. So in Harry's modest way, he went on to extol the virtues of why there was no one better for the job than Harry Caray.

Andy McKenna was floored, but he hung up the phone and immediately picked it up again and called Jim Dowdle, and Dowdle didn't hesitate. He had known Harry since the early '60s and was always a friend and a big fan. Much more importantly, I believe Dowdle felt as though Harry was probably the best salesman of baseball that ever came down the pike. And in turn, he believed that there was no better salesman for the Chicago Cubs and their cable superstation than Harry Caray.

So Dowdle moved quickly and hired Harry almost on the spot. Harry was to be the point man in a war to win baseball fans in Chicago and all across the Midwest. And I'm sure that Jim Dowdle never once regretted his decision to bring Harry aboard for the 1982 season.

Problem was, Milo Hamilton was the most surprised man in the world when it happened. There's a famous picture of Milo at the press conference when they announced Harry's hiring that shows him clearly stunned, angry, and in denial. And that really started the acrimony between Milo and Harry. Understand, though, that it all went one way. It wasn't between Harry and Milo; it was Milo's anger directed at Harry.

Milo never forgave Harry for getting the job he felt was rightfully his. Had the Wrigleys not sold the club but instead continued their ownership, Milo certainly would have had the job—maybe for life. But life takes strange turns. This one turned against Milo and toward Harry, who went from a lovable local broadcaster on the South Side, playing before small crowds and a tiny TV audience, to a national cult hero because of WGN's nationwide signal and the lovable Cubbies on the North Side of Chicago.

This gave people a chance to see him sing and dance and cheer on the Cubs. And in the years in which they were bad—which were most years—it gave Harry three hours to talk about the shrine known as Wrigley Field.

"What a wonderful thing it would be," Harry would say, "if you could plan your summer vacation to Chicago around a trip to Wrigley Field. The ivy, the lake, the scoreboard, the green grass, the Budweiser. Hey, Arne, show the boats out on the lake."

Now, the only way you could see a boat from Wrigley Field was if you were an eagle, or if you were sitting on the roof. But that didn't matter. It didn't matter that most of what Harry said was simply a salesman selling his product, because it didn't sound like that.

"Hey, Arne, show me the sailboats," Harry would yell out over the air.

"Harry, it's 40 degrees out there," Arne would say into his ear. "There's not a boat in sight."

So there was Arne panning Lake Michigan, looking for a lonely boat out there. You could almost hear Arne in the truck scrambling for a shot of a sailboat in some canned footage.

"Harry," I'd say, "who do you think is sailing out there, the Loch Ness Monster? The wind chill is 10 degrees."

But Harry was brilliant. He sold the team, the park, and baseball—and sold Chicago, too. People would come from hundreds and sometimes thousands of miles away. Regardless of how the Cubs were doing, there was no better place to spend a summer day.

"Come to the ball game and have a Budweiser and then hang around the neighborhood and go to one of the many local establishments and have another Budweiser," Harry would say, never passing up an opportunity to plug Budweiser.

People think he promoted Bud all the time because they paid him to be a spokesman, which was only partially true. Sure, he did pretty well with that "Cub Fan, Bud Man" routine that lasted a few years. Really, he was pumping it up because he probably owned more stock in the company than anyone but the Busch family. As a young man, Harry bought a lot of the stock on his own, and it made him a very rich man. Like everything else with Harry, he was self-made. Nobody gave him that stock. He invested in it and made out like a bandit.

I used to tell him that he could live until he was 400 without running out of money. I know one place he didn't spend his money was on clothes. As Jack Buck once said, "Where do you spend your money, Harry? I know you don't spend it on clothes because you dress like a flood victim."

But I digress. (How unusual, huh?) Back to Milo and Harry.

I'll never forget the day Milo was walking up the ramp toward the press box, and a young boy chased him all the way to the top, yelling, "Milo, Milo, Milo!" The kid finally reached him, all out of breath, and handed Milo a ball and a pen.

As Milo began to sign, the boy said, "Milo, do you think you could get me Harry Caray's autograph?"

That was pretty much the extent of Milo's popularity once Harry took over at Wrigley Field. And because of that, Harry and Milo got along like Clinton and Starr, which opened the door for me.

The WGN folks started looking to do two things: They wanted to move Milo over to radio, making him the No. 1 voice; and they wanted to find a real baseball analyst to sit next to Harry on TV. That way, Harry and Milo would never work together again, which was all due to Milo's inability to get along. If not for that, they might have kept the two of them together for years and years.

This way, Harry called the first three innings and last three innings on TV and the middle three on radio, while Milo did just the opposite. I stayed in the TV booth for all nine innings, and the only time Milo saw Harry was when they passed on the ramp between innings. So in 1983, they hired me to keep the two of them from killing each other and at least thirty feet apart.

The rest is history—except for the part about Milo's jealousy.

Toward the end of the magical 1984 season, Milo was still miserable. Not even a divisional title—the Cubs' first title of any kind in thirty-nine years—and Ryne Sandberg's MVP season could placate him. He just couldn't get over the fact that he'd been promised the job and then had it taken away from him.

There was a lot of backbiting and a lot of sniping going on, but it was only going one way. Harry would've been content to leave Milo alone, stay out of his way and go about his business, even though he knew Milo couldn't stand him. But Milo had a world of animosity toward Harry, so after the '84 season, the Cubs made a change.

To this day, Milo says Harry got him fired, but I know this: Had Milo just done his job, he might still be here today and might be the guy who eventually succeeded Harry. But he couldn't help himself. He had this great job as the No. 1 radio voice of the Cubs, but it wasn't enough for him.

The Cubs had no burning desire to get rid of Milo, but he couldn't handle Harry. And Harry didn't get him fired. He didn't think Milo was significant enough to do that. In the end, the Cubs actually did Milo a favor, because if they had gone outside of baseball to get an announcer, Milo might have been out of a job. Instead, they took Dewayne Staats from Houston, and Milo got Dewayne's job with the Astros.

Milo used to call Harry "the canary" because of Harry's singing prowess, and once he arrived in Houston, he took it a step further. When the Cubs were visiting the Astrodome, Milo would stand up and rock back and forth, pretending to be drunk and singing during the seventh-inning stretch, a completely classless act.

After he left Chicago, Milo spent the next fourteen years ripping Harry, and kept right on going—even after Harry died. To anyone who cared to listen, he spewed his vitriolic soliloquies and to this day remains a bitter man. Anyone that knows the history of WGN broadcasting knows Harry and Milo didn't get along, but it was pretty much a one-way feud. Still, there comes a time when you should call it a day, especially when one of them happens to be dead.

He could have said something like, "Nice talking to you. Good luck wherever it is you're going and hope you got what you wanted out of life." But Milo didn't take that approach. I think he viewed it as a debate in which the last person talking got the most points. Well, Harry was dead, so Milo kept on talking.

What's stunning is the fool he made of himself after Harry passed away. White Sox owner Jerry Reinsdorf was not on very good terms with Harry, to say the least, but he had the good taste to issue a very plain but respectful and honest statement congratulating Harry's career and his great contributions to the game of baseball.

Milo could have done that. But he didn't. He couldn't help himself.

He even came in and screamed at Chip Caray one night in Houston in 1998 because he felt like the fans were paying too much attention to Chip and ignoring Milo. Chip handled it much more diplomatically than I would have—and certainly in quieter fashion than Harry's son Skip, who is just looking for a chance to pop Milo.

The night Jack Brickhouse died, Skip made a point of mentioning it on the air on Atlanta's WTBS superstation, which was a very nice gesture. And after a fine tribute to Brickhouse, a Hall of Famer in his own right, Skip finished and said, "I wonder what Milo Hamilton thinks about that."

The thing is, Harry would have been the first to tell you that there were more than a few people who didn't think the sun rose and set on his very existence. But everyone except Milo had the common sense and the common decency to acknowledge Harry's career and his dedicated love of the game.

Milo didn't feel it necessary to do that. I think Milo felt like he could throw a knockout punch without expecting one in return because Harry was dead and couldn't respond. It turns out, though, that Milo was vilified for the things he said and in that sense, Harry got the last word anyway.

Wild About Harry

You can forgive Milo Hamilton for one thing: He, like many others, came through Chicago thinking he was the heir apparent, but they all went bye-bye eventually. The list is long, but little did anyone know that Harry's successor was coming to all of the family meals in Atlanta for the past twenty years.

Milo was hardly the only person who could ever claim to dislike Harry Caray. But the numbers on that side were infinitesimal compared to the millions who loved him. Harry had fans everywhere and in every way. They came in big packages and small boxes. They were rich and famous and poor and infamous.

And sometimes, they were simply out of this world.

At least once a year, we'd be having drinks and Harry would tell me the story of how he met Elvis Presley. And the thing is, I never got tired of hearing him tell it.

"I was doing a basketball game for the St. Louis Hawks, who are now in Atlanta," Harry said. "We played eleven straight games on Mondays in Memphis to try to promote the team, and when I was there I'd get a lot of calls at the hotel from Cardinal fans, because that was big Cardinal country down there.

"We had a lot of our young players come through Memphis, so we had a big following. Well, on this one Monday, I was at the hotel getting ready to go to the arena when the phone rang and a nice young man on the other end said his name was Elvis. And he went on to tell me how he'd been listening to me for years on the radio and how much he liked the way I call baseball, and so on and so forth.

"So I say, 'Thanks a lot, buddy, but I gotta get going because I have to go to work.' And I was about to hang up when the guy says, 'Harry, I don't know if you heard me, but this is Elvis, Elvis Presley.' I said, 'Yeah, right. You're Elvis and I'm the president.'

"I was going to hang up and he says, 'Harry, what city are you in?' I said, 'Memphis.' He says, 'Harry, it's really me, Elvis Presley.' I said, 'Prove it.'

"So he tells me to go downstairs in ten minutes and he'll pick me up. So I went down to the lobby and out the front door. And sure enough, here comes a Cadillac and after it parks, out from behind the car steps Elvis Presley. THE Elvis Presley. I couldn't believe it.

"I said, 'My God, it's really you.' So we shake hands and he asks me to come over to the house, to Graceland. I said, 'I'd love to. I just have to get my briefcase.' So I went back up to the room and got my briefcase and we drove over to Graceland.

"We talked for a few hours and had a great time, but I had to get to the arena. I tried to talk him into coming with me to the basketball game. I was thinking about the great ratings we could get with him there doing the broadcast with me, but he said, 'Harry, they've got a brand new fieldhouse down there and they'll tear it apart if I show up. No, I'll wait for you here and when the game's over, I'll send a car for you.'

"So he arranged to have me picked up afterward and brought me back to Graceland."

As you can imagine, these two men were made for each other. They sat up all night drinking and talking and having fun with various "associates," before the King realized something important.

"He says, 'My gosh, Harry, you haven't eaten, have you?' I said, 'No, Elvis, I forgot because we were having such a good time.' He was worried because I hadn't had any dinner," Harry recalled. "So at about 4 A.M. he calls this place that stays open all night for him, and he orders up a barrel full of ribs and some chicken, and we sat around and drank Budweiser until the sun came up.

"He played his guitar and we sang songs and there were some attractive young people there, I'll tell you that much. This was Elvis with a thirty-inch waistline at about twenty-three years old. It was a sight to behold."

Well, a couple of years went by and Harry was vacationing in Las Vegas when he drove past the Riviera Hotel and saw Elvis' name on the marquee.

"You know in our business, Steve, you never know how people are going to react when they don't need you for something," Harry said. "Everyone in the world is your friend when they need to plug a record or a TV show or a movie or something, but you might see them a week later and they act like they've never met you before.

"So when I walked into the Riviera Hotel, I didn't know what to expect. But I gave the bellhop twenty bucks and I said, 'Get a message to Elvis that Harry Caray is down in the lobby and let me know what he says.'

"Ten minutes went by and I was starting to think he wasn't going to answer my note when I got paged over the loud-speaker. 'Harry Caray, please pick up phone bank No. 16.' Sure enough, it was Elvis.

"He says, 'Where are you?' I said, 'I'm in the lobby.' He said, 'Come on back.' I said, 'Back where? I don't know where you are.' So he tells me to stay right where I am. He said he'd come get me. Well, I'll be a son of a gun but all of sudden the elevator opens and out walks Elvis Presley, the King of Rock and Roll. He comes out in cutoffs with no shoes and people are mobbing him. But he was very polite to everyone.

"Then, he grabs my hand and takes me back to his room and we spent the whole night together. I watched his show and he mentioned me on stage and had me come up and say a few words, and we saw the sun rise together. What a marvelous young man he was, and that's unusual in that business."

Harry often said that the day Elvis died was a very sad one for him and everyone around the world, but I don't think Harry ever realized how similar the reaction would be in the baseball world when it was Harry's turn to go.

Harry could never escape from the fans, not that he really wanted to, but there are times when you need a little privacy.

He told me that when he was still working in St. Louis, he was in a bar one night and went into a bathroom to relieve himself. When the guy standing next to him saw Harry, he got so excited that he turned around to shake Harry's hand, and urinated all over Harry's pants and shoes. So from that day forward, Harry was always very careful about shaking hands with guys in bathrooms.

As you might have noticed, Harry had a habit of overstating things.

I remember he used to say to me, "Steve, what Italian do you think sang in front of the most people last year?"

I don't know, Harry, you tell me.

"Why it's me, of course!" he'd yell with delight. That might not have been exactly right, but he was the same guy who was upset when they took sixty-two games off of WGN-TV in 1998 and put them on a local cable outlet in Chicago called CLTV, because he thought WGN was missing the boat.

"How in the world could they preempt me for *Buffy the Vampire Slayer*? I'm prettier than she is," Harry said. "Everybody knows that."

Well, maybe not everyone.

One guy Harry would have stepped aside for was Frank Sinatra—maybe the only person Harry actually idolized or was in awe of.

"You know, Steve, it's just like the song," Harry said. "Frank did it his way and I always did it my way, and that's why I have so much respect for him. We both were married a few times and we both had our tough times. We both grew up in poverty.

"But Frank always did it his way and I've always done it my way. I never worried about getting fired or getting in trouble because of the things I say. That's what I love about Frank. He doesn't care what people think about him and he doesn't always say the 'right' thing, if you know what I mean. But he says what he thinks. He has friends people don't like, but he says, 'To heck with what people think,' and he keeps company with who he wants to keep company with. That's what I've done and I think people appreciate that kind of honesty and loyalty." Specifically, Harry was talking about Sinatra's alleged mob connections.

"Steve, I talked to Frank about that many times," Harry said. "He swore to me that all that stuff was a bunch of crap. He said he had friends that might have been on the dark side, if you will, but they were his friends. What was he supposed to do, not have friends? Or check with everyone to see if it was OK every time he made a new friend?"

You see, that was what amazed me about Harry. On the one hand he was so opinionated, but on the other hand he could make it seem so simple and be so forgiving. That's how he felt about friendship. He sure wasn't going to have anyone tell him whom he could have as a friend.

When Frank died in May 1998, the first person I thought of was Harry. I know that news would have made him very sad, too. Harry appreciated great entertainers, and there was probably none greater than Frank Sinatra.

How popular was Harry in Chicago? Well, one night in 1989, the Mayor of Rush Street returned home to the Ambassador East hotel after a night out with Cubs public relations director Ned Colletti, and ran into a bit of a problem.

It was a bus, actually.

The bus stopped in front of the hotel just as Harry was getting out of his limo, and the riders on the bus went nuts. People wouldn't sit down and the bus driver couldn't move with all of the hysteria. So Harry did the only thing he could do.

He got on the bus through the front door and walked down the aisle high-fiving and shaking hands with every passenger on the bus, until he finished and exited through the back door. And as the bus pulled away, the happy fans serenaded him with "Take Me Out to the Ball Game."

How many other broadcasters in the history of the world would draw that kind of response?

Cubs first baseman Mark Grace says the thing that separated Harry from the rest of the world's broadcasters was his monstrous popularity. When he thinks about it now, Grace is still amused by the sight of Harry's annual spring training grand entrance.

"It was usually around March 1 and the rest of us had been there for a few weeks already when Harry would show up," Grace said. "He would wait until about 12:30 when HoHoKam was good and packed and fans were hanging from the rafters, and then he would emerge from our dugout and the place would go nuts.

"The shocking part is me and Ryno and Andre would be out there signing autographs and Harry would walk out of the other dugout and everyone would go running over to him. The three of us would be left standing there talking to each other and giving each other autographs. It was the most amazing thing. But that's how big Harry was.

"Ryno and Ernie Banks are probably the biggest stars in team history and when Ryno was here, he was the show. Andre was absolutely adored by the fans, too, but it's hard to think of anyone bigger than Harry. I mean, when he entered a stadium or he walked into a room, everything stopped.

"To this day, when I think about that I'm still amazed by it."

Harry was also a very big fan of Mark Grace and I think those words would have made him very happy.

Another guy Harry liked was Bill Murray, a huge Cub fan and one of our guest broadcasters when Harry was sidelined by the stroke in 1987. Murray put on a fabulous show that day. But, some people—not me—thought he crossed the line, and some were concerned that Harry would find it offensive.

"To the contrary," Harry said when he returned. "I watched it that day and I thought he was great. I loved it. It's what I've always tried to be. His approach was like mine, though mine was a little more refined. I feel like yelling at the other team, too. I want the Cubs to win, but I like to see good baseball and if a player on another team makes a great play, I say that." As good as Bill was, Harry wanted me to know he was still better.

"That was great for a day," Harry said. "But I don't think you could take 162 of those."

If you watched Harry at the ballpark every day, not one passed without a visiting player coming up and throwing his arms around the "King of Rock and Rum." There were two main reasons for that. One is that he rarely criticized opposing players the way he did his own guys, and they also knew he could be very kind to them on national TV if he wanted to be. Those players all had families watching them play and often the WGN games were the only ones mom and dad could see.

"Visiting players seem to like me more than the Cubs players do," Harry told me. "Our guys get mad at me when I say they lost the game, but what can I do? If you throw the ball away and the other team scores the winning run on that play, should I lie about it?

"What happens is people come up to them every day and tell them what I said on the broadcast instead of hearing it themselves, and then they get mad."

That really drove Harry nuts. He wouldn't even talk to a guy if he said he heard it third-hand. He would only discuss the situation once the player saw the tape.

"When I first started, Steve, it was more difficult to do my type of broadcast and tell the truth all the time," Harry said. "Back then, no one dared criticize a player or an owner or a general manager or a coach. That was taboo.

"But the thing is, when I'm critical it's not because I'm trying to be mean. I'm just telling the truth, like any fan would tell the truth. I can't sit there and pretend it's OK when the guy at home knows it's not OK. How does that look?

"The thing is, when I say an error cost them the game, I'm not the one who gave the error. That's the official scorer. I've always told the players: don't even talk to me about something you think I said until you hear what's on the tape. Then we'll talk. Invariably, they'd come back and say, 'What you said is fair. You just said what happened.' And I'd say, 'That's right. That's my job.'

"What I've always found, Steve, is that the great players never have a problem with you telling the truth on the air, because they know they made a mistake. No one has to tell them that, and they don't care that you said they made a mistake. And the guys at the end of the bench, they're more realistic than anyone. They know they're lucky to be there. But it's the guys in the middle, the guys trying to get on the field that have the biggest problem with the truth.

"But there's a reason they're not on the field, and that's really what they can't handle. When they yell at a broadcaster, usually they're just mistaken about where their anger should be."

The man was like a walking encyclopedia of broadcasting, baseball, and psychology all rolled into one.

People often wondered how he could stay out with Elvis to see the sun rise, broadcast the next day as if he'd gotten a good night's sleep, and still explain Broadcasting 101 as if he was an eighteen-year-old. The truth is he could keep up a pace that no other human could imagine, but he didn't do it every single night.

"I wasn't drunk every night," Harry said when we would talk about his prime drinking years. "I couldn't do that and continue to do baseball every day, especially day baseball. The tales are widely exaggerated. I might go out every night, but that doesn't mean I'm drunk every night. I might even stay out late every night, but it doesn't mean I was blind and couldn't see."

I think part of it was Harry had built up such a tolerance that most people probably figured he had to be drunk because a mere mortal would be after that many drinks. And he was so popular, that people bought him drinks everywhere he went, but that also doesn't mean he finished each one.

His good friend Pete Vonachen often says that Harry was never in a bar long enough to get drunk. "We'd go to a place and by the second drink he'd be restless and want to go somewhere else to see where the action was," Pete said. "We left full drinks on bars more often than we finished them."

There was no one more popular in baseball broadcasting than Harry when he was a radio star in St. Louis, because he was really a radio star all over the Southeast, Southwest, and Midwest. In fact, some people would go so far as to say he's responsible for baseball's popularity throughout those regions of the country because he was their first link to baseball's excitement.

In many places there was no team for the fans to go see, but they listened to Cardinals baseball and Harry made them love the game. I still run into people today who tell me about how they grew up listening to Harry call baseball in Alabama, Texas, or Arizona.

"Steve," Harry explained, "St. Louis was the southern-most team in the major leagues when we had 175 radio stations on our Cardinals network and there was no TV. So I was as big in Miami as I was in St. Louis. The Cardinals were the team of the South and the Southeast and the West. Of course, in the Midwest the Cardinals were hugely popular. So I never felt the need to go for that 'network stardom,' even though I got lots of offers.

"I had a chance to go with Mel Allen but I didn't want to be a No. 2 guy when I could be No. 1 in St. Louis. I had chances with other New York teams and with network job offers, but I thought I'd be in St. Louis my whole life. I didn't think I'd ever leave there.

"But beyond that, why would I go to a network and work once a week when I have seven days a week in St. Louis, and later in Chicago? What would I do the other six days a week? I was getting in too much trouble when I was working every day. I can't imagine what kind of trouble I'd be in if I worked only once a week."

When Harry did get fired in St. Louis in 1969, there were wild rumors about how he'd had an affair with the wife of Augie Busch III. Harry always denied them, but he thought it was great that someone would think that.

"I'd rather have people believe the rumors and get fired than have the job and have people not believe it," Harry explained with classic Harry logic. "Here was a twenty-four-year-old beautiful starlet married to a billionaire, and here I was a broken down old guy in my fifties already. I'd rather have people believe it. It was good for my reputation."

How popular was Harry?

When he joined the White Sox, he signed the first contract in broadcasting history that had an attendance clause in it.

"They said they couldn't pay me what I wanted because they couldn't afford it," Harry told me. "So they offered to give me $10,000 extra for every 100,000 people we drew over 600,000. I took it.

"Well, the first year we did 900,000 so that was an extra

$30,000 and the next year we did 1.2 million so that was $60,000 more and the year after that we did 1.3 million.

"That's when they called me in and said we're putting you on straight salary before you put us out of business."

In 1997, we had an event in Chicago that featured President Clinton and the First Lady. Just as you would expect security was very, very tight—until Harry came walking in.

Three guys had been specifically watching three doors in one particular hallway and when anyone went near them you would have thought the world was coming to an end. They wouldn't allow anyone near those doors. But all of a sudden, Harry appeared and all three guys dropped what they were doing and went nuts. "Hey, it's Harry Caray," one of the guys yelled, and they all came running to him.

At that moment, anyone could have walked down that hallway and the Secret Service never would have even known. That's how big Harry Caray was.

One of my favorite Harry stories actually comes from the days when he was announcing basketball.

"I was in New York for the NIT tourney before baseball season started and I figured it was time to really see the part of town I'd never seen," Harry told me. "So I went to Harlem and told the cab driver that I wanted to go to a black club where I could hear some real music.

"He thought I was nuts but he brought me there and I have to tell you, Steve, I got a lot of stares from people there. I asked for the manager to come to my table and when he showed up I said, 'Look, I want to see Harlem. My name is Harry Caray and I'm a baseball announcer from St. Louis, in town to do some basketball. If you think I'm in trouble here or if I'm causing trouble, I'll leave.'

"He said, 'I know who you are and this is no trouble. I'll sit right here with you.' And I stayed until 2 A.M. and he brought four beautiful women to the table to sit with me. We had a great time and after he closed up, the manager said, 'Do you want to see Harlem for real?' I said, 'Yes,' and so he took me for a ride. We got out of the car and walked down a dark alley and to an old, quiet building.

"He said, 'Walk up these stairs and I'll follow you.' Now this was about a 6-foot-9, 300-pound black guy behind me and I was starting to think I was in big trouble.

"Steve, the guy says, 'Stop here.' I thought I was done. I thought no one would ever find me here. All of a sudden, he rings the doorbell and a little window opened up. The guy gave the password, the door opened and it was like Mardi Gras in there! There was booze and gambling and girls and the place rocked with music all night long.

"This guy, I wish I could remember his name, took me to about six different places and we stayed out until dawn. It was one of the best nights I ever had in my life, if not THE best."

CHAPTER 16

The Man, the Mirth, the Legend

think because he was an orphan, Harry was very respectful and was very serious when anyone brought their parents into the booth, and that was the case when he saw my folks. Before my mom died in 1984, he always went out of his way to see them when they were in town and mention them on the air and invite them up to the booth.

After my mother passed away, he was no less enthusiastic about asking my dad and my step-mom to drop by and he was always reverent in his treatment of my father, Paul. I think he made my folks feel very special and feel very welcome in the booth, a courtesy he did not extend to everyone, let me assure you.

But he went out of his way, I think because he didn't have that stable family life growing up. He appreciated the relationship I had with my folks and to him that was sacred. When players asked him to say hello to their parents on the air, he made a big deal out of it.

When Michael Jordan's father, James, made a habit of dropping by the booth during the 1992 and 1993 seasons, Harry made a very big deal out of it because he was so happy that Michael was so close to his dad. And he did that any time he could because it was something he missed out on.

◆❖◆

He was born Harry Christopher Carabina in St. Louis on March 1, 1914. And not long after that, he was an orphan.

In the late '80s, I asked Harry to take me back to where he was born in St. Louis and tell me the story of his childhood. He wasn't crazy about the idea, but he did it anyway. We spent an entire off-day together, and I'll tell you the parts that I think he would have wanted you to know.

"I never knew my father, Steve," Harry told me. "He left when I was born and I never met him. I never knew what he did for a living. I don't know what happened to him. I don't know when he was born and I don't know when he died.

"My mother's name was Daisy Argint. She remarried when I was about six and died when I was about eight. The only memory I have of my mom is of her dying. I remember the doctor placing a mirror over her mouth and saying she was gone. That was about 1921 or '22. The doctors quite obviously didn't know then what they know now. They didn't even know what she died of or when she died until they used that mirror.

"My stepfather ran a restaurant and he wanted to keep me, but he couldn't take care of me. So I was sent to live with my mom's brother, and he was married to Doxie Argint, my aunt.

"Not long after I joined Aunt Doxie, who already had four kids, her husband disappeared or died. We don't know for sure, so I was raised by Doxie alone.

"I sold newspapers as a child and made a few pennies a day, and I would go to a lending library where I could rent a book and get a chocolate marshmallow sundae for three cents and I would read half the book. The next day I would come back and read the rest of it. I think this is how I became so well versed on so many subjects."

Harry didn't let his guard down often, but on this one particular day he did.

"You know, I consider myself tough, Steve, but I cry at movies when I see someone in pain," he said. "I can't stand to see sick people or sad people. I'm invited to hospitals all the time but I can't take it. I don't go. I send money instead. I just don't like seeing sadness.

"My own childhood was so sad. When you don't know your mother or your father or any of your relatives, it's a tough road to hoe, and I hoed it."

Harry didn't tell me these things to make me feel sorry for him. I think it was his way of trying to bring us closer together, so that in our tough times we would understand each other a little better. Like I mentioned before, it was like a marriage, and he was trying to give me something on which to base our friendship.

It was tough for him to talk about these things and he didn't speak much about them publicly because he wanted no sympathy. Harry's belief was that everyone has problems. Here he was a rich and famous man, and he didn't want anyone to think he had a bad life, because he thought he had a great life.

"This was a cobblestone street," I recall him saying as we walked down the avenue. "Now it's obviously paved.

"I played baseball right there on that corner and I was pretty good, believe it or not.

"From here you could get the street car and go to the old Sportsman's Park and pay half a buck to get in and ten cents for a hot dog. I would eat outside the park because it was a nickel cheaper than inside.

"After the game I came home and played ball. The kids played ball all day and half the night. We were all neighbors and that meant something back then. There was more friendship and guys were pals. The neighborhood was a family type thing. We played ball together. You don't see that anymore in the neighborhoods.

"Progress is not always a good thing and part of it now is you see kids watching TV twenty-four hours a day. Or they're playing basketball. Everyone wants to be Michael Jordan, which isn't a bad thing. But kids don't play baseball anymore. You don't see them walking to the neighborhood park and playing ball like we did all day. You don't see ball fields hardly at all, and when you see them, they're empty.

"I understand why you would want to be Michael Jordan. Who wouldn't? There's nothing wrong with having dreams. I can tell you because I dreamt and some of my dreams were realized, too."

Harry showed me the shoe factory where he sold newspapers when he was eight years old, and he showed me the school he attended, which brought back more sad memories.

"In grade school I had no white pants. We couldn't afford a pair," Harry said. "The other kids teased me mercilessly because they all had white pants. One thing I can't stand to see is kids being teased. I get furious, because I felt that pain."

Harry never wanted credit for it, but he spent thousands of hours and raised millions of dollars for charity, and it usually involved children's causes and orphanages. One of his favorites was certainly Maryville Academy in suburban Chicago. He never got over the pain he felt as a child, and the only way he could try to make it better was to help kids who were going through the same things he went through.

He tried to hide it his entire life, but inside that tough old son of a gun was a little boy who still felt the pain of loneliness and poverty. That's something I tried never to forget.

When Harry graduated from high school, the University of Alabama offered him a baseball scholarship, but he couldn't afford the books and room and board. He also had no way to get there, so he turned down the free schooling and went out to make a living.

It's now a famous story about how he sent a letter to Merle

Jones, who ran KMOX in St. Louis, and got himself a tryout at the station. Harry told him he wanted to broadcast baseball even though he'd never done a broadcast or seen a studio in his life. He just knew he loved baseball and thought he could be more exciting than the men he heard on radio.

And he was right.

"I believe in the land of opportunity, Steve," Harry would often say with a smile. "Because it happened for me. Something good always happens out of something bad, and even though my childhood might not have been the best, good things happened to me because I learned how to survive and fight for myself."

In his later years, Harry freely admitted one thing. "I wasn't a very good father, Steve," Harry said. "I was on the road all the time and I didn't know what it meant to be a father, maybe because I never knew a father figure in my life."

And now that I think back on it, this may have been the only time Harry used the word "regret" when he was talking about himself.

"I've made a lot of mistakes, especially with my children," Harry said. "But you know, you can't change what you've done. You just try to make up for it any way you can and I think I've done that. And I've also tried to tell my grandkids not to do the things I did.

"I didn't see my kids grow up. That's my biggest regret. But I didn't have parents, so I didn't know. Maybe that lesson is the best thing I can give back."

Harry had five children and Dutchie had five, and he treated her kids as if they were his own. In the last six or seven years of his life, Harry made a lot of changes, and I think Dutchie's influence was enormous in that respect.

Not until he was nearly eighty years old did Harry Caray

finally believe he was part of something most of us take for granted.

"Steve, the first time I ever felt like I had a family was on Christmas in 1994," Harry told me during the summer of '97. "I had everyone out to Palm Springs and we had the best time with all the children and grandchildren.

"Steve, I used to sit home and cry every Christmas because I never had a family, but that all changed when I saw Dutchie's mom and dad die. I realized I had so much there for me that I should start to be a part of a family. I never knew how to do that until I learned from watching Dutchie.

"I never really knew my kids. I didn't know how to know them and I didn't know how to be a dad. I had no role to follow. People talk about role models, well, I didn't have any. All I knew was everyone left me. Well, I've changed all that."

Harry made no secret of the fact that the greatest thing that ever happened to him was broadcasting a game with his son Skip and grandson Chip. It thrilled him that all three had made it big in baseball broadcasting.

"Of all the things that happened to me," Harry said, "the thing I'm proudest of is having all three of us in the game."

I'm warmed by the closure Harry got on some of those issues in what turned out to be the last few years of his life. He got a chance to love a family and be loved in return.

The last time Chip spoke to him was on the day before his fatal accident. Harry was so excited about Chip joining him in the booth in Chicago for the 1998 season, and the last words out of his mouth as the conversation ended were, "I love you, Chip, and tell your dad I love him, too."

To Your Health

When Harry came back from his stroke in 1987, he wanted Dutchie to travel with him because she helped him out so much, and without her he wouldn't have been able to get through the days.

But Harry lived the vagabond baseball lifestyle that Dutchie had never experienced before. I think it was tougher on her than it was on him, even though he was the one who had suffered the stroke and was many years older.

Harry came back on May 19 and by the middle of June, he was getting stronger and more like his old self with every passing day.

Dutchie had been with us the entire time, and by the end of the season she was exhausted. I can remember her sitting in the back of the booth always doing her knitting, but the poor woman looked so tired. Any human being would have been exhausted following Harry until 3 A.M. every night and watching a last-place team every day.

I remember thinking to myself that Harry looked great and was getting stronger and healthier by the minute, and I had no concerns about his survival. On the other hand, I was worried about whether Dutchie would survive. But she did, and in the process she did a phenomenal job of taking care of Harry, as she did that year and for every day of the rest of his life.

Harry never would have made it to age eighty-three without her support and comfort the last few years. She began traveling with him again the last four years because Harry said he "didn't want to die alone in a hotel room, like Don Drysdale did in Montreal."

Of all the things Harry ever said to me, those words might stick out in my mind as much as any.

Now as you know, Harry wasn't one to admit that maybe he had lived a little too hard, but in the years after the stroke I think he realized that he was mortal after all.

"Maybe in the final analysis, the stroke was a suggestion that I was going too far," Harry said. "Maybe that was a warning from upstairs that I had to back off a little bit."

Harry backed off completely for a while and then when he felt 100 percent again, he went back at it 100 percent. He attacked the old lifestyle that made him famous, and without any moderation.

And he went on fine like that until June 23, 1994, when Harry walked out of an ice-cold clubhouse and into the vicious heat and humidity of Miami. As he neared the playing field, Harry collapsed in a heap and hit his face on some stairs.

Stunningly, he was hardly injured from the fall, suffering a bloody lip and scratch on his nose and some broken glasses. But it was the reason for the fall that caused so much concern. It didn't receive a lot of notice at the time, but Harry suffered a ventricular tachycardia, or irregular heart rhythm, that probably caused him to black out and fall down. That may have been the exact same thing that occurred the night he fell in Palm Springs on Feb. 14, 1998. But the difference in Miami may have been that there were paramedics only a few feet away when it happened.

On that day in 1994, I was surprised when I got word in the

booth about an hour before the game that Harry had fallen down. I didn't know if he had slipped again and hit his head or fallen for some other reason.

Harry never had heart problems before that. He'd had the stroke and some stomach problems, but I'd never heard about any heart trouble. It wasn't on my mind so when someone came up and said he'd fallen down and was on his way to the hospital, I figured he must have hit his head. I didn't know until later that he had an irregular heart rhythm.

I did the game myself that day and it was pretty strange. I didn't realize how serious that situation was, but the doctors knew immediately. And unlike the stroke, when Harry started drinking again and staying out all night as soon as he felt up to it, this time he had no choice. If he didn't stop drinking, he would die, and this was one of the few times in his life he took the message to heart, no pun intended.

After that fall, he never had another drink and I know he truly missed that. If he said it once, he said it 1,000 times: "Steve, I wish I knew when I was going to die, because I'd like to have two martinis that day." That was a big part of his life and it really made him happy. I personally didn't think that he could do it, but he drank non-alcoholic wine and beer until the day he died.

Was Harry the same broadcaster at eighty-two as he was at forty-two or even seventy-two? No, but it didn't matter, either. Because Harry was more entertaining than 99.99 percent of the people in the business and the fans worshipped him.

That's why Jim Dowdle, the Tribune Company exec who hired both Harry and me, told me more than once that Harry had the job forever if he wanted it.

Over the last few years of Harry's life, Dowdle—who delivered a fabulous eulogy at Harry's funeral—often could be heard defending Harry and suggesting that in today's antiseptic world of broadcasting, Harry would never get hired.

"Did he get slower? Sure he did. Did he mispronounce names? Sure he did," Dowdle said. "But he always did that, and 95 percent of the Cubs fans forgave him when he did that and the other 5 percent didn't like him in the first place.

"I just don't think there'll ever be another broadcaster who brings color to the game and relates to the fans like Harry did. He did such a wonderful job of bringing the game to the fans."

As the No. 2 man at Tribune Company, Dowdle had the power to make and break careers, but the thought of replacing Harry never once entered his mind.

"I thought it was his job to say when he didn't want to do it anymore," Dowdle said. "I respected him. He would have had to say, 'I don't want to do it anymore,' for me to make a change.

"He earned that. He was one of those few guys, like Michael Jordan, who can say that. I think you let them tell you when they're done.

"The amazing thing is he never lost his enthusiasm, which is usually what finishes those guys. Harry went up there every day like he was a twenty-three-year-old guy just starting out.

"He always was excited to broadcast the game and even in down years he always felt like that was the day the Cubs would win and turn it around. I'll miss him a lot as a friend. The game will miss him even more as a broadcaster and an entertainer."

The part that hurt Dowdle the most I think is that Harry's grandson, Chip, was going to join us in the booth in 1998. Harry wanted him to take over the family business, if you will.

"Harry was so excited about his grandson joining him and then taking over, that I think it's appropriate that Chip get to do that," Dowdle said. "I'm comfortable with that. I think Chip's comfortable with that. Let's let nature take its course.

"There can never be another Harry, but it makes me feel

good to know Chip will be in the booth. Harry was so excited about him taking Harry's place someday, that it just feels right.

"People will say, 'He's got the same last name but he's nothing like Harry.' Of course not. No one can be like Harry. No one will ever again be like Harry."

As great as it was working with Harry, I never made a secret of the fact that I wanted to become a major league general manager, and Harry was totally supportive of that.

"Steve," he said, "if you've got a dream, then you have to pursue that. Me, I don't want to do anything but broadcast Cubs games. There's no other job in the world I would want. But you need to try to reach out for whatever you think is out there for you."

So I never made any important professional decisions without consulting Harry, because he always had a good business sense when it came to finances or baseball or broadcasting or anything. He had a great innate sense for those things, and I always listened to what he had to say. I'll miss dearly the opportunity to call upon his wisdom, because while he tried to make everyone think he was common, his intelligence was anything but that.

One of the results of his stroke was that he may have sounded more common than he really was. I remember a particularly poignant night in 1988 when the two of us went out in Montreal and got to talking about that night's game and how we both felt that he hadn't had a particularly good game. I think he was starting to feel some of the effects of the stroke and maybe wasn't able to do all of things that he used to do during the course of the game.

People who are younger or people who have just plain forgotten might not know that in his prime Harry was an absolutely brilliant and exciting broadcaster, as good as anyone in the history of baseball. But after the stroke, there was a change.

"Harry," I said, "when the game's on the line, you are just as brilliant as you've ever been in your life. That hasn't diminished in any way."

"But Steve," Harry pleaded, "I'm trying just as hard when the Cubs stink."

"I know you are, Harry," I said. "But I think when it counts, you're concentrating more, because you get all of the names right and your call is brilliant and you're at the top of your game. You're still wonderfully dramatic and your call is exciting."

"Well," Harry laughed, "I don't think the Cubs are going to get much better any time soon, so I don't know what we can do about it."

"Maybe one of the ramifications of your stroke is that your mind wanders a little bit more when it's as dull as a desert out there on the field," I said. "When the game's on the line, you paint a beautiful picture. Even when you're screaming and yelling, everything comes out right. It's fantastic. Maybe you just have to concentrate and think about the game a little more and I'll help you do that when they're losing 12-2."

It was really quite a night because it was one of the few times we spoke to each other as though we were on equal footing. He really wanted and needed my help. There wasn't much I could do for Harry anywhere outside the broadcast booth, but at least inside the booth, I could still help him call the game.

That's something that makes me feel a little bit better during those moments when I miss Harry the most.

A Perfect Day

On Sunday morning, Feb. 15, 1998, I went out to play golf in Scottsdale, just as I do on most mornings during the off-season.

I was on the links with a friend of mine, Don Vogel, who happens to be a robbery-homicide detective in Mesa. He had one of those electronic pagers that carries all of the news on them. We got to the fourteenth hole at about 10:15 A.M., and as Don checked the headline news, his jaw dropped.

Vogel didn't say a word. I knew it was something major by the way he was acting. He just turned and showed it to me and I began reading it:

"Harry Caray is in critical, but stable condition after collapsing at a restaurant in Palm Springs, California."

Although it was certainly surprising, at that point I didn't think there was cause for alarm. I knew someone his age would be listed as critical any time he was taken to a hospital, and when I saw that he was stable, I thought maybe he had fainted or something like that.

You have to remember that Harry trained me to get used to his falls and pratfalls, because he bounced back quickly from the very serious ones and the not-so-serious ones. I figured he'd be up and around in a couple of days, and it never dawned on me that he was in trouble.

"He'll be here in Arizona in about two weeks," I said after reading the news. "He always comes out right around his birthday, March 1, and I'm sure this won't change his plans."

I was fully intending to see him either the night he got in or the next day at the ballpark. It never occurred to me that he was really sick or that he wouldn't make it to spring training. The word "stable" really threw me off.

And again you have to understand that for those of us who saw him on an everyday basis for so many years, you reached a point where you honestly believed he was going to broadcast forever.

I would sit in the back of the bus with Arne, Barry Rozner, Mandy Cohen, Thom Brennaman, Joe Cornejo, and a few others, as we went back and forth to the stadiums or from one city to another. And whenever the subject of Harry's health came up, we talked in terms of Harry calling games in 2025 while the rest of us were off babbling to squirrels in the park.

You can joke about it to a point, but you become desensitized and start to believe it because he had overcome so much. He had outlived all of the terrible things that would have killed a mere mortal. He had beaten the odds more times than a professional gambler. I just assumed Harry would be there in spring training. We would open the season together in Florida with his grandson Chip in the booth, and Harry would be truly elated.

I wasn't at all emotionally or psychologically prepared for what was to come.

We came to believe he was Superman. We joked about it so often and spoke about it so frequently, that there came a point in time when we began to believe that Harry Caray would live forever.

And after a while you just kind of forgot that in our midst walked the Elvis of broadcasters, the Michael Jordan of the baseball world, the Pope of the Cubs. And you forgot that he was on "borrowed time," to use his own words. You forgot that he'd had a stroke and that he had heart disease and that he was eighty-three years old.

And you forgot that in 1994, he suffered an irregular heart rhythm in Miami that could have killed him.

I witnessed so many of his dangerous and life-threatening falls through glass tables and down stairs and through windows, that I just plain forgot that he was human.

The first time that I realized that it was much more serious than everyone was letting on was when I called the family home in Palm Springs later that Sunday night. I spoke to Harry's stepdaughter, Muffy, and she told me that the tests were not revealing a lot of brain activity. The news they were already receiving from the doctors' preliminary tests was that the parts of the brain that contain the mental faculties were really not responding at all.

And I was stunned. I got off the phone with Muffy and I just sat in my house alone. In silence.

I kept thinking that it's just a dream and that I'll wake up and Harry will be all right. But it wasn't, and I didn't know how to react. I still had a hard time believing that it was happening, and a large part of me kept saying, "He's come back from serious traumas before when no one gave him a chance. Maybe he'll do it this time, too."

But a bigger part of me already knew he was gone. Muffy said he was in a coma, and I knew that it was very serious. I knew this was probably going to shape up as the biggest battle of his life, in a lifetime full of big battles. What I didn't know at that moment was that this was one he had already lost. To the best of my knowledge, he never regained consciousness after his fall at that night club on Valentine's Day.

And I have to believe that if you're in some sort of a holding pattern talking to God, and He'll cut you a deal whereby you can go back, but you've been unconscious for too long and you can't broadcast anymore, I know Harry would have said, "To hell with it. Let's take a walk. It's been a good life. Let's call it a day."

Harry wouldn't want to come back if he couldn't call a game again. That was more than what he did for living; that was his life. Without that outlet for his thoughts and feelings and opinions, Harry would just as soon be dead. I know that because he told me that.

I could never imagine him not broadcasting. I knew he would never retire voluntarily. I always thought it would take something catastrophic to take him out of booth, and that's what it took.

We all knew that Harry would pass away someday, but you never think it's going to happen now. Much like a baseball career that you know will come to an end someday, you just don't believe it'll be this year. I knew Harry would go one day, but I stopped thinking about it. I didn't think it would happen in 1998 or 1999, and next year I would've thought the same thing.

The man was indestructible. I saw him fall twenty times. I saw him come back from a stroke and a heart problem. He was run over by a car in St. Louis and had both his legs broken. But he always came back.

This time, he didn't. He never regained consciousness. Harry Caray died on Feb. 18, 1998, at the age of eighty-three.

The baseball world shuddered.

A country mourned.

A family wept.

And I cried.

Harry's son Chris had a sense of humor much like his father's, so it didn't surprise me when I spoke to him shortly after Harry died and he immediately made me laugh.

"Steve, you know what it would have been if he had come out of that coma?" Chris asked.

"I don't know, Chris," I said. "A miracle?"

"No," Chris deadpanned. "It would have been the ultimate mulligan."

This is the same Chris of whom Harry used to laugh and say, "I have the only son in his forties who's retired. He's retired because his father keeps on working. I'd like to quit, but I have to support my son."

Dutchie Caray said the most upsetting part of the entire ordeal was the constant phone calls from media at her home and at the hospital.

"Steve," she said, "you wouldn't believe what went on. They tried a lot of dirty tricks to get information. You wouldn't believe it. They would call the hospital and pretend to be me or one of the kids, trying to find out what was happening.

"One time I was sitting right at the nurse's station when the phone rang and someone claiming to be Dutchie Caray wanted to know how Harry was. That was pretty upsetting.

"There were a lot of things reported that were wrong, too. I think it's just a shame that someone wants a story that bad. This was a person's life."

There are stories that need writer's embellishment. And then there are the Hollywood movies that need none at all.

Harry Caray's life was just that. With every day that he lived beyond his stroke in 1987, Harry was a walking, breathing, imbibing embellishment, so no one need put a spin on his life.

Nor on his death.

Just as you would hope, Harry Caray went out having spent his final hours on this planet in candor and splendor, with a nearly perfect day and a spectacular night.

"I'm telling you that his last day here was beautiful," Dutchie said. "He had absolutely a fabulous day."

Harry had to go out in a blaze of glory, and glorious was exactly the way Saturday, February 14, 1998, could have been described by everyone around him. Harry's final hours on earth were on that Saturday because he really wasn't with us after that.

"It was the most wonderful day," Dutchie recalled. "Two of his grandchildren were here visiting for a week before we left for spring training, and Harry just loves his grandkids.

"The fifteen-month-old, Caitlin, she adored Harry. She would crawl over to him and say, 'Papa, up.' And she put her arms up like she wanted to be picked up. And he would do it over and over and over again, and they would laugh and laugh.

"He'd get down on the floor and crawl around with her. Oh, he had a great time with the little ones, and they loved him.

"On that day, it was almost like Caitlin knew something was going to happen. She never left his arms. She kept crawling up to him and saying, 'Up, Papa, up.' Maybe she knew.

"Caitlin loved Harry. And those little ones really brought a change in Harry the last few years. You'd look over and see Harry feeding one of them with the bottle and the rest of us would look at each other like, 'Wow.' He never did that kind of thing before in his life and never knew he was missing anything. Now he wanted to do it and he enjoyed it very much.

"I think he was reaching out for a piece of his life he never had experienced before and trying to grab all that he could grab as fast as he could do it."

That was important for Harry as he tried to bury his own mistakes.

"He took care of all of that," Dutchie said. "He never had a family as a child and he didn't know how to be a part of one. But he learned and he loved it."

And he made up with his five kids from an earlier marriage, including Skip, who went years without a serious father-son relationship. For the last few years, Harry flew the entire clan to Palm Springs for Christmas, giving him the holidays he never had as an orphan.

Even better was that he treated Dutchie's five children as if they were his own. All together, they had fourteen grandchildren and one great-grandchild.

"The last few years of his life were very peaceful and pleasurable," Dutchie said. "He had nothing to feel bad about."

Especially not his final night, which was spent with the love of his life, dining and dancing at a local restaurant on—what else—Valentine's Day.

"We had the best time," Dutchie said. "We danced and we sang and we had so much fun. Harry felt great. There was nothing wrong with him. It was a wonderful night.

"What people maybe don't know is that Harry's health was terrific. If he hadn't fallen down, who knows how long he might have lived."

Exactly how, why, and what happened at that restaurant isn't important now, but the fact that he went out in style is. His last act was to acknowledge his fans with a wave, as a nightclub singer sang his praises. Harry couldn't have written the script any better than that.

"He had such a wonderful life. He had a great life. What more can you ask?" Dutchie offered rhetorically. "He used to say, 'Dutchie, I've been so lucky. I've had so much fun and lived so well. I've nothing to be afraid of.'

"I'm sad, of course, and I'll miss him dearly. Every minute I'll miss him. We were best friends. But I'm not upset. He had a great night and I knew it had to happen sometime. I didn't want it to happen, but nobody lives forever."

Dutchie was spectacular throughout the ordeal, always worrying more about everyone else than herself, always trying to make everyone else feel good, and never letting on that she felt the pain.

Some have said that Dutchie is just as tough as Harry, and now we can see it to be true. And what we would have thought was the toughest decision of her life, turned out to be nothing of the sort. Knowing Harry's soul was already gone, allowing his body to follow was the only possibility.

"It's the easiest thing I've ever done," Dutchie said. "If you could have seen him that way, you wouldn't have wanted to see him. To go in the hospital room and have it be so quiet. I mean, he always had the TV on and now there was no TV. It wasn't even him.

"We would have done it sooner, turned off the machines, but we were waiting for the rest of the family to get here in Palm Springs. Once Skip got here, we all said our good-byes.

"It was a blessing, because no one would have wanted Harry to live like that, especially Harry. He's at peace, and so am I."

This amazing woman said she really managed to hold it together, except for a time the night Harry passed away, when a Palm Springs TV station flashed Harry's picture.

"We got back from the hospital and my little Caitlin saw Harry's picture on TV. She crawled over to the TV," Dutchie said. "She pointed to the TV and said, 'Papa, Papa,' and gave us a big smile. That got me pretty good right there, because I knew she'd never . . . you know."

Yeah, Dutchie, we know.

CHAPTER 19

Take Me Out to the Funeral

As the day of the funeral approached, those of us closest to Harry spent hour after hour and day after day telling stories and reminiscing about our time with him.

One of the more emotional moments was when I had dinner with my old partner, Thom Brennaman, who remembered the day he told Harry he was leaving Chicago. Thom never wanted to leave the Cubs and Chicago, but faced with growing pressure from his Chicago bosses to give up the stardom associated with network TV, Brennaman felt like he had no choice. And late in the summer of '95, he also knew it meant telling Harry Caray he wouldn't be coming back.

"I went into his booth and told him what was happening and said it was time for me to move on," Brennaman recalled. "Well, Harry threw his arms around me and started to tear up, which, of course, made me start to tear up, too.

"He said, 'I'll really miss you, Thom. We've had a lot of fun together, but you're doing the right thing. This is the best thing for your career and you know that.'

"All that time I had wondered if I really was doing the right thing. Harry wanted me to take over for him when he left, and here he was saying, 'Don't look back.' After hearing that from him, I knew I had done the right thing. If ever there was a guy who knew about taking chances and making tough decisions, it was Harry. And once I was done talking to him, the doubt immediately vanished from my mind."

Thom went so far as to credit Harry with taking his career to another level after he arrived here from Cincinnati in 1990.

"He treated me like I was his own grandson," Thom said. "He looked out for me when I came to town, when I didn't know a soul. It was a big city and a big-city job and he took me under his wing and he went to bat for me, time and time again."

But it was the personal side of Harry that Thom said was hardest to imagine living without.

"He was a dear, dear friend and I really loved him," Thom said. "It's hard to believe there will ever be another Opening Day without him."

One of the best lines came from Arne Harris, when he heard the reports that business at Harry's restaurant went up 150 percent in the week after Harry collapsed and died.

"I just believe that if the doctors could have gotten that message to him, that would have woken him up for sure," Arne said. "Not because of the money, but when he heard all those people were there, he would have wanted to be there, too. Harry never wanted to miss a party, especially if the party was for him."

The funeral was held on February 27 at Holy Name Cathedral in downtown Chicago. It truly was an event to be remembered. Harry was sent off with a presidential ceremony and everyone who was anyone in Chicago attended.

Dutchie received a letter from Bill and Hillary Clinton and

a phone call from Vice President Al Gore. Illinois Governor Jim Edgar and Chicago Mayor Richard Daley attended, along with many celebrities and athletes.

Among them were many players who thought of Harry as their very own, like Hall of Famers Bob Gibson, Billy Williams, and Stan Musial; future Hall of Famer Ryne Sandberg; stars like Rick Sutcliffe, Mark Grace, and Sammy Sosa; broadcasters Jimmy Piersall, Bob Costas, and Brent Musberger; Northwestern coach Gary Barnett; and Chicago icon Mike Ditka.

I was a little surprised to see Mike fly in from New Orleans, where he was quite busy trying to put together a football team, but Mike said quietly, "I just thought I needed to be here to pay my respects. I can't say it any more clearly than that."

My lasting memory of the trip will probably be the plane ride in from Arizona on the Tribune Company's corporate jet, which carried Scott Servais, Grace, Sosa, Andy MacPhail, Dr. John Marquardt, Jim Riggleman, Yosh Kawano, Billy Williams, and me.

It's a ten-seater and whenever we hit some turbulence, we felt every inch of it. But in the last hour, we hit some real bad weather and—needless to say—the fellas were getting a little nervous. Mark Grace and Sammy Sosa are nervous flyers to begin with, so they were holding onto their seats and Grace and Sosa both looked as white as a sheet.

And the whole time I was thinking about Harry and laughing out loud.

"The ironic part," I said as we were bouncing all over the sky, "is that I've never worried much about flying, but if we do go down in flames going to this funeral, Harry is going to meet us when we get up there and he's going to have one hell of a laugh at our expense.

"Harry will say, 'There's no way I would've come in for your funerals, so you guys are idiots for coming in for mine, and now you're dead'."

And I could hear him screaming with laughter.

But we made it safely and spent a good deal of the flight talking about Harry and telling stories and laughing constantly. Harry touched a lot of people's lives and everyone who knew him had at least one definitive story to tell. He had that magnetic personality and you couldn't help but have some interesting or funny or controversial story that in some way directly related to you.

I don't think anyone who ever came into contact with Harry was ambivalent. People loved him or liked him or hated him or respected him or laughed at him. I think that's a great measure of a man. Harry would tell you that indifference was the thing he disliked the most. He had a definitive opinion on everything—even things he knew nothing about—and the last thing he wanted was someone who didn't care about Harry Caray one way or another.

"Love me or hate me," Harry would say. "Just pronounce my name correctly."

As shocked as I was by the amount of luminaries from all walks of life gathered at Holy Name Cathedral, I was more stunned by the fond farewell that everyone gave Harry. It was much more like a celebration than a funeral.

When everyone stood on the advice of Maryville Academy's Father John Smyth and gave Harry a standing ovation, there was suddenly a loud knocking noise coming from somewhere in the Cathedral. Then, during the brilliant and entertaining eulogy delivered by Pete Vonachen, again the noise returned. No one could identify the knocking sounds, and I turned to Pete's son, Rocky, and said, "I'm pretty certain that's Harry trying to get out." When he saw the crowd and all the laughs everyone was having, Harry wanted to be part of it.

The persona of Harry being so indestructible and strong, I believe most of the people gathered there in the church expected him to walk out and be resurrected in time for Opening Day.

As funny as Pete was that day, I'm surprised Harry didn't feel upstaged and join the party, but as Pete said, "I sure hope there's no resurrection, because none of us can go through this again."

Pete said it wasn't easy being Harry Caray's best and life-long friend. "There were several qualifications," Pete said. "You had to have unlimited stamina, a cast-iron stomach, your bag packed, and your divorce lawyer on retainer."

And then Pete reminded us that Harry was concerned about what would happen when he died. "I hope they don't cremate me," Harry told Pete, "because I'll burn forever."

Harry would have loved the day. It was a tremendous cele-bration of the life of a man who lived life as a celebration.

Harry always said that when he died, he wanted Dutchie to throw the greatest party ever and put it on Harry's tab. "That's all I want," Harry said. "You handle everything else."

So that's exactly what she did.

Immediately after the funeral, we all made our way over to Harry Caray's restaurant and had a ball—not to mention many a cocktail. We toasted Harry with Budweiser and everyone told stories. They ranged from the wild to the mild and from the obscure to the obscene. The important thing is that we laughed. Everyone thought of at least one truly funny line.

From Mark Grace it was the memory of Harry Caray in 1995, as he introduced the starting lineup. "There's Luis Gonzalez in left and Brian McRae in center and Sammy Sosa in right, and in the infield, Mark Grace at first, Rey Sanchez at second, Shawon Dunston at short, and Todd Zeile at third," Grace recalled. "Behind the plate it's Scott Servais, and on the mound is Steve Trachsel . . . who's having a TER-R-R-RIBLE year."

From Rick Sutcliffe: "We're on the plane one day in 1984 and Harry sends someone back to get me. I'm thinking, 'Oh, no. What have I done?' But I get up to the front and he says, 'Sut, you're 12-1, and it looks like you're gonna win the Cy Young. Are you for real or is this some kind of fluke?' And he starts laughing. We had a bunch of drinks that night."

And from Billy Williams, remembering a particularly bad Cubs team in 1994: "Our outfield had a little trouble catching the ball, so they kicked it a few times. We were getting beat pretty bad. Harry had about all he could take after another error and on the air he says, 'Boy, oh boy, what a *lousy* ball club!' Only Harry could say something like that about his own team and make people laugh."

But I thought of what made Harry the happiest, and that was the Cubs winning the National League East in 1984. "That was probably my greatest joy in baseball," Harry told me one night at dinner in 1997. "I want to jump up and down when I think about that, and I want to cry when I think about Steve Garvey. That ball Tim Flannery hit through Leon Durham's legs, how can that happen? You know how? Because that's baseball. That's what makes the game great. It happens every day. The impossible is possible. The unbelievable is believable. That's why I love baseball."

But I think the memory I'll carry with me forever from that day is that of the organ music as we followed the casket out of Holy Name Cathedral. It was "Take Me Out to the Ball Game," and it took me a second to recognize what it was. When I understood what was happening and as we reached the doors and Harry made his final exit, I lost my composure and started tearing up.

Harry had beaten me again.

The 10th Inning

told Harry over and over again that I thought he'd be dead for two years before he stopped coming to the park, just based on eighty-plus years of inertia. I figured the team doctor would have to tell him he was dead and I expected Harry to argue with him.

"Harry, you've got no heartbeat," the doctor would say.

"No, you're wrong," Harry would reply. "I want to do a few more games."

People who knew Harry felt that when God came to take him, he'd swing some kind of a deal to get one more ball game to call. Maybe he did that already, in 1987 or in 1994, and just didn't tell anyone about it. The way he scripted his exit in 1998, you'd swear he had the whole thing planned, like part of the deal was that he could pick the day and time.

On Valentine's Day, with his sweetheart Dutchie, at one of his favorite restaurants, waving to a cheering crowd with a nightclub crooner singing, "My Kind of Town." It was the only fitting way for Harry to go out.

Really, it was a perfect day.

One of the funny things I thought of while I pondered Harry's ultimate fate, was the conversation we had in 1994

about what would happen to him when he was gone. We were having dinner on the road and talking about what would happen when he passed away. I mentioned that the life expectancy of a man who retires at sixty-five was twenty-seven months, because retirement is hard for most people to live with. With nothing to do, life doesn't have a purpose for some retirees.

"Harry, if you're physically able to broadcast, why would you ever think of retiring?" I asked.

"Well," Harry said, "there's been times when I thought that if the Cubs could win the World Series, maybe then I'll retire. Sometimes this is just too tiring for me, so I thought maybe I could get to the point where I could retire."

"Harry, I just can't imagine you in retirement," I said. "Cut back the schedule and do fewer games per year, and you can work more years that way. Working half the time for ten years is better than all of the time for five years, know what I mean?"

"I do, Steve," he said. "But how do you know they'll let me do that?"

"For God's sake, Harry, you can do anything you want," I said. "They need you associated with the broadcast until the Cubs get good, and that could take forever and a day. Until that time, the Cubs are selling Harry Caray and the ivy.

"Besides, you can't walk away from the microphone. What are you going to do, broadcast breakfast with Dutchie every morning? For one thing, she would probably kill you, and secondly, you'd probably lose your mind from boredom. So as long as you can physically get to the booth, there's absolutely no reason for you to retire."

Harry was a professional celebrity, and broadcasting baseball was his life. I was sure he'd never die during the season because I was sure his will was too strong to allow him to give it up while baseball was being played.

And I'm sure now that Harry never would have retired. I think he would have done home games forever, even if he could have only done an inning or three, especially the seventh, eighth, and ninth.

But one day I said, "Harry, I have an idea I'd like to run by you."

"Sure, Steve," he said. "I'm sure this will be a beauty."

"I know that when you go, you'll rest in peace," I said, "but the seventh-inning stretch is one of the great bits in baseball history and the Cub fans need you up there. So when you do go, I was thinking I could still have you up there with me."

"Steve, you know I'll be with you in spirit," Harry said. "And with spirits, if you know what I mean."

"I know, Harry," I said. "But I was thinking more along the lines of having you stuffed. You know, like Roy Rogers had Trigger stuffed. I'll take care of you. I'll dust you off every couple of days. And the best part is we can hold you up during the seventh-inning stretch and sort of wave you at the fans. What do you think?"

I never did get an official response from Harry on that one, but I have a feeling he was taking it under advisement.

Since Harry passed away, I've been asked probably thousands of times about what I'll remember most about our years together. That's one of the reasons I decided to put these thoughts down on paper. For nineteen-plus chapters now, I've told you many a story that I'll never forget, but here's another crack at some of what I'll remember about Harry Caray:

I'll remember his belief that something good always came out of something bad. "I never thought I'd leave St. Louis and the Cardinals, Steve," Harry said. "After twenty-five years with the team, that was a terrible day in my life. But something good always happened to me after something bad.

"That's the way my whole life went. I lost the Cardinals but eventually I wound up with the Cubs in Chicago. I had a terrible childhood, but a great time as an adult. I never really had a family, but then in my later years I had a wonderful family. Out of bad can always come good if you look for it."

I'll miss his outrageous behavior and hysterical antics, which didn't end even as he got older. I remember a day in '94 when the game was crawling at a snail's pace, and the pitcher was throwing to first and taking forever between pitches. All of a sudden, I hear this snoring noise, and it's Harry pretending to fall asleep on the air.

"You're not sleepy, are you?" I said.

"How could you not be?" he replied.

I laughed so hard I had to turn off my mike. He was still right on the money with his commentary.

Some broadcasters have a problem being entertaining when the game needs a push, but that's when Harry was at his best. There were times I thought I'd like it to be calm, but now that he's gone, the world is way too quiet a place.

I'll remember his generosity and that Harry paid for everything every time we ever went anywhere. I can count on one hand the number of times he allowed anyone in his company to pick up a check.

I'll remember that when Mandy Cohen organized my fiftieth birthday party at Harry's restaurant, Harry insisted on picking up the tab for the entire night—and that was no cheap evening.

In each of the last three years of Harry's life, I celebrated my birthday at his place and he picked up the tab every time.

I'll miss the Christmas hams he sent every year. Whenever

I got it, I knew we were about halfway done with the off-season and that spring training was right around the corner.

I'll miss his infectious laugh.

I'll miss his passion.

When he was mad, he certainly let you know he was mad. When he was happy, he was uproariously happy.

I'll miss his storytelling, not just because he was a great storyteller, but because Harry in his own way had lived so much baseball history that he was a great historian and keeper of the game. He was a museum of pennant races and World Series heroics, not to mention great players. Because he began as a radio man, Harry told stories with color and vigor, and you almost felt like you were living through it when he painted a picture.

I'll miss his irreverent humor and his grasp of the ridiculous.

I'll miss the outrageous things he said that only he could get away with. A younger or less charming man would have been tried and convicted on the spot for sexual harassment or even worse. But because it was him, people would throw their palms up, shake their heads, and say, "That's Harry."

I'll miss the way he dressed, which was just about the worst anyone could possibly dress. Harry was color blind and I used to remind him of that every morning at the ballpark.

I'll miss his constant hacking and his penchant for coughing into my mike while sitting on his cough button.

I'll miss the way he walked, which made him look ridiculous, and the way he talked, which made him sound outrageous.

And I'll miss the fact that he never complained about his constant pain. While people decades younger than him always found a reason to whine, Harry was nearly always jolly and happy to be at the park. And only a few of us knew that he was almost always in pain. Harry couldn't walk without agony because of his terrible back and leg problems, but he never said a word. If he stood or sat for too long, he was in constant pain, but he never said anything.

I'll say it again: He was the toughest son of a gun I've ever known.

I'll miss the way he moved when he was younger. He never stayed in one spot too long, because life was out there waiting for him and he wasn't going to waste too much time in any one place.

I'll miss that he never wanted to sleep, because he was afraid he might miss something.

Since Harry died, people have stopped coming up to me to ask, "Where's Harry?" But I think I know where he is.

Right now he's having a beer, watching a game, picking a fight with Ben Stein, arguing about who drank more, yelling at Charlie Grimm, and wondering out loud why Grimm's Cubs never won a World Series. And he's having a martini with Billy Martin, whom he wished had managed the Cubs to a World Series.

I know he's looking down and I'm sure he's got that knowing smile on his face, at peace with the fact that his grandson is sitting in the seat he occupied for so many years. And I know he's wishing that his grandson will do something he was never able to do, and that's broadcast the Chicago Cubs in a World Series.

A lot of people probably think we went through heir apparent after heir apparent. But here's a guy—to use Harry's phrase—who carefully orchestrated his entire career, and took himself from the absolute depths of an orphaned childhood to the pinnacle of baseball and broadcasting immortality. In the end, you wonder if he didn't just decide that he wouldn't give up his chair until he could be certain another Caray was sitting in it.

So "Where's Harry" today?

Smiling.

As it happened for the twenty-five years I knew him, when it came down to the final act, Harry once again had the last word.

Just like he always did.

I once asked Harry how he'd want us to remember him.

"Steve, I hope people will say, 'The Cubs just won a World Championship and isn't it a shame that Harry wasn't here to see it?' Because that would mean they've finally won," he said. "I don't want there to be any one memory, really. I think fans realize that we all come and go. Players, owners, broadcasters, we all come and go, but the game lives on. People love the game and the love of baseball should never die. That's what I want them to remember. I hope to God the people that run the game never kill it, and I hope people remember that it was the fans that I really cared about."

When I think of players like Stan Musial and Ryne Sandberg, it reminds me of the final words he said about Musial when he retired.

"Take a good look, fans," Harry said, "take a good, long look, because his like will never be seen again."

He said similar words about Ryne Sandberg when he retired in 1997, and when I think of those words, it reminds me of how much Harry loved the game. That part makes me sad because few people have ever loved anyone or anything the way Harry loved baseball. Now that he's gone, I just hope he has found a way to watch baseball again.

"Steve," he once said, "if I can't watch baseball after I'm dead, it's just going to kill me."

And now, I think it only appropriate that I leave you with Harry's own words from the final wrap-up of his last game in 1997, as we said good-bye to each other—and another losing season—looking forward with hope to spring:

"This is Harry Caray, speaking from Wrigley Field, and God willing I hope to see you next year, and maybe it'll be the next year we've been waiting for forever.

"So long everybody!"

Epilogue

The 1998 season turned out to be a magical one for the Cubs as a team and for Sammy Sosa and Kerry Wood as individuals. And that led a lot of people to wonder if Harry had something to do with what was happening on the field, as if he were directing traffic from above.

After every home run, Sammy would point to the sky in tribute to Harry, which was a brilliant and poignant gesture. Maybe Sammy really felt like Harry was along for the ride in 1998, or maybe he realized how much Harry had done to help him become a fan favorite at Wrigley Field. But I know what Harry Caray would have said if someone suggested to him that he or his late, great friend Jack Brickhouse had something to do with the Cubs' success after their deaths.

"How in the world can a dead guy help the Cubs win games?" Harry would have asked. "You want to know what wins games? I'll tell you what wins games. Pitching wins games, and scoring more runs than the other guy wins games.

"That's how you win games, not because of some goddamn help from another planet. When did you ever see a UFO pitch eight innings of three-hit ball or smack a two-run home run?"

Harry and I used to argue all the time about how to build a baseball team. I, naturally, have always said that you win with pitching. Over the course of several years, the teams with the pitching will generally win out over those that don't have it. In my mind, it begins and ends with starting pitching. Harry, on the other hand, liked offense and he liked home runs. In 1998, the Cubs got a lot of both.

One of Harry's favorite sayings always began with, "Honesty compels me to report to you . . ." And so in honor of Harry, honesty compels me now to report that Harry would not think much of the idea that he had some kind of heavenly clout. He would be very flattered to hear people say he had that sort of influence, but he would have thought it a bit silly.

Harry forgot more baseball than most people will ever learn in a lifetime, and Harry would be the first to tell you that if you don't have the horses, all the other-worldly effort won't do much for you.

Still, there was magic in the air all season long in 1998, and Harry's presence was definitely felt.

Cubs marketing director John McDonough—who invented such concepts as the fan convention and brought Beanie Babies to baseball—came up with the fabulous idea of "guest conductors" for the seventh-inning stretch.

Not only was it a huge hit, but it also brought back fond memories for me of the 1987 season, when we had celebrity guests in the booth every day, helping me out until Harry returned from his battle with a stroke. But there was a catch: Unlike 1987, I was pretty certain this time that Harry wasn't coming back.

For the rest of us, the season of learning to live without Harry Caray ended with the Braves' sweep of the Cubs in the playoffs. But for Dutchie, the education continued in a quiet apartment where there was once so much commotion.

"To tell you the truth, there are still days when I forget for a split-second," Dutchie said. "I think, 'Well, Harry ought to be getting home any minute.' And then I catch myself, and it's kind of sad.

"When you're with someone for so long, you look forward to certain things, and the best part of my day was when Harry got home from the ballpark and we'd go out to dinner or some-place fun. I have to catch myself sometimes and remember that he's not coming back."

As do we all, but for Dutchie Caray the reality hits home a little harder. In fact, the tremendous joy she felt during the Cubs' sensational 1998 season was sometimes tempered by thoughts of what might have been.

"I think the thing that really goes through my mind most often is that Harry missed out on his chance to broadcast with his grandson, Chip. He was so looking forward to that," Dutchie said. "He talked about it all the time and he was so glad Chip decided to come to Chicago. He really wanted to call the games with Chip, and he thought it was going to be a real-ly fun summer."

And what a summer it was. Can you imagine Harry Caray experiencing the thrills brought to Chicago by Sammy Sosa, Kerry Wood, and the miracle Cubs?

"I do think about that and for a minute or two I get sad and I think, 'Why not one more year?' But it passes," Dutchie said. "But on the other hand, when you reflect back on his life, Harry had such a great life and you can't ask for too much more than that. He was so blessed and blessed and blessed.

"He had a fantastic life and he accomplished so much and experienced so much, that I sort of think that you just can't ask for more. You never know what God's plans are for us. But whatever our plans were for Harry, they weren't the same as God's plans for him, and you just have to accept that."

Of course, you'd have a hard time convincing some Cub fans that Harry didn't have a direct impact on the 1998 sea-son. After all, it certainly seemed as though they were getting some heavenly intervention when the ball got stuck in the vines. And when it got stuck under the wall-padding. And when it ricocheted off of Rod Beck's leg and right to Jose Hernandez in San Diego.

All of those plays and others like them saved Cubs victories, and it had the masses looking skyward.

"I kind of laugh when I hear people say that, but then, who does know for sure?" Dutchie said. "If we all knew for sure what life was like in the beyond, we all might be fighting to get there. It might be wonderful. But we don't really know.

"I don't put a lot of faith in that kind of talk, that Harry had a hand in all of it, but on the other hand, the Cubs were pretty amazing and you kind of had to wonder sometimes what was going on.

"It was such an emotional ride and there were so many low points and high points. It was a real roller-coaster ride all summer, and every time you thought they were done and our hopes were dashed, they came up with another miracle. Who knows, maybe Harry was up there pulling some strings."

Dutchie, meanwhile, has become the matron saint of the Cubs since Harry's death, and her sudden status as a public figure has grown to proportions that she can't possibly understand.

"I get recognized by everyone, everywhere I go and I'm amazed by that," Dutchie said. "No one really knew me before Harry died but now everyone stops me and says, 'Are you Dutchie?'

"I'm fine with it. It's really not a problem, but it shows you the power of TV. It's amazing to me that so many people recognize me. But it's kind of like I'm carrying the ball for Harry and it gives people a chance to express their sorrow when they see me."

Indeed, Dutchie's omnipresence in 1998 gave the city of

Chicago and Cub fans everywhere an opportunity to love and remember Harry whenever they saw Dutchie. And she handled her duties with spectacular grace and loving care.

"From the minute Harry fell in that restaurant on Valentine's Day to now, the reaction to his passing has been just unbelievable," Dutchie said. "Harry knew he was popular and I knew he was popular, but I'm sure neither of us knew it was anything like this.

"Every day, people still come up to me and tell me how sorry they are and how much they miss him. It's mind-boggling to me how many lives he touched. It's just beyond anything I could have imagined."

If there was anyone who didn't recognize Dutchie before Opening Day, 1998, they certainly did afterward, because she began the guest conductor series by leading an emotional crowd through the singing of "Take Me Out to the Ball Game." That might be Dutchie's lasting memory of 1998, because she still has nightmares about it.

"Well, I can't sing and I can't believe I ever agreed to do it," Dutchie said laughing. "But when Harry passed away, the Cubs were so good to me and I told them that if there was anything I could do, just ask. So John McDonough called and asked and I agreed without even thinking about what I did. About three days later I thought, 'Oh my God. What the heck did I do? I can't sing in front of 40,000 people.' But it was already announced and I was stuck. It was two weeks of agony waiting for it to happen.

"I was so nervous and I know it was awful. I know I can't sing. But Harry probably would have liked it because he couldn't sing either."

And, of course, that was the whole point of the guest singers. The worse, the better. Harry liked entertainment, and the seventh-inning stretch in 1998 not only became a lasting and memorable tribute to Harry Caray, but it was also astoundingly entertaining.

◆❖◆

There have been some positives for Dutchie, who made many new friends and developed some very strong bond.

"I got a lot of support from Ryne and Margaret Sandberg," Dutchie said. "We've become very close and they were very, very supportive. They came and stayed with me at the house a few times and that was great. They're very nice people and I know Harry and Ryne were very close, so it made me feel good that they spent a lot of time with me."

But the relationship that Dutchie never could have predicted was the one she now has with Chip.

"Chip and I didn't really know each other very much until the 1998 season, but I've really grown to admire and love Chip," Dutchie said. "He's one fine young man who really loves his wife and daughter. He's crazy about them, and that's so nice to see these days.

"I'm really so happy that we've developed a friendship, but it's also another reason that I'm sad that Harry wasn't here to be a part of it."

So even though 1998 brought Dutchie so much joy, there's not a day that goes by without some sorrow.

"I think about Harry every day and I go to church almost every day and I pray for my family and for Harry," Dutchie said. "I do think about him and I pray that I get through the day. It's comforting for me.

"But my friends, and Harry's friends, have kept me so busy that they haven't let me get lonely. And I was at the ballpark a lot and that was so much fun that there wasn't time to be lonely."

But it was the fans who made life tolerable for Dutchie. It was their support and their outpouring of affection that gave her the strength to get through the rough times.

"It's just been really comforting and a warm feeling to know they really liked Harry that much," Dutchie said. "I'm at a loss for words when I think about that. What can you say? All I can say is thank you to the fans. I have no other way, other than to express my sincere thanks to them.

"From the bottom of my heart, thank you Cubs fans for loving Harry and for not forgetting him."

The good news was Chip Caray signed on for his first tour of duty in Chicago and he had a spectacular debut in the booth. Chip nearly took the job in the fall of 1995 when Thom Brennaman left Chicago, but because of financial reasons and other career considerations, Chip turned down the WGN offer. Harry was very, very disappointed because he was sad Thom was leaving, and he very much wanted Chip to take the No. 1 chair and become his heir apparent.

Because of that, things were a bit strained between Harry and Chip for a while. But when Chip decided to take the job in the winter before the 1998 season, that was truly one of the happiest days of Harry's life. He envisioned himself broadcasting as long as he physically could, but calling fewer and fewer games each season. Then, there would be a passing of the torch to Chip as his role expanded over the next few years.

He was still contemplating exactly how Chip would fit in when Harry passed away and left us with little to debate. Chip would be the No. 1 man, period, while continuing his studio hosting duties for Fox baseball on Saturdays. Instead of Chip calling seventy or eighty games like Harry had planned, Chip would be in the big chair for nearly all 162 of them.

And from Chip's point of view, there probably couldn't have been a more difficult way to get thrown into the job. He expected to have a great time working with his grandfather and getting to know him better over the next few years. At the same time, he could ease into the No. 1 role.

Jay Leno, for example, had time to ease his way into the

role while hosting hundreds of shows over the years before he took over for Johnny Carson. He also had a definite date that he knew about a year in advance.

Chip didn't have those advantages, and with his hectic schedule, he basically arrived on Opening Day in Florida with no chance to prepare for his new job in a seat Harry was supposed to keep warm for him.

It couldn't have been much tougher.

The hard truth is that no one knew what to expect from our new partnership, least of all Chip and I. But there was enormous pressure on Chip because of the sheer enormity of Harry's life and death. Chip was under a microscope and the critics were looking for a chance to take their shots.

But from Day 1, it was like Chip and I had been teamed up for years, and even one of our bosses came into the booth in August and told us that from the beginning, it sounded like we had worked together for years.

You might be surprised to read that the first time we ever discussed the broadcast was when I rented a car on Opening Day in Miami and gave Chip a ride to the ballpark. As we got close to the stadium, I said, "By the way, what do you do?"

"I'm Chip Caray," he said. "I'm your new partner. Nice to meet you."

"No, seriously," I said. "How would you like to handle this? I can't dictate the broadcast because you're the play-by-play guy, so it's pretty much up to you to decide the tempo."

"Well," Chip said. "I think it's my job to describe the action and bring the analyst into play. I like a conversational broadcast and I like to have some fun. There's a time to be serious, but I believe we're here to entertain the fans first and foremost, while informing them at the same time."

And that was the only time we discussed our new partnership, but it worked out extremely well. Not only did we have
great chemistry right off the bat, but we were also very fortunate to have the 1998 baseball season as our third man in
the booth.

Here we were, thrust into this partnership without knowing
a thing about each other, and we were entrusted with taking
the team through one of its most exciting seasons ever.

You never know how it's going to work until you sit next to
each other and see how the other guy reacts, but from my
standpoint it was almost like slipping on a very comfortable
pair of shoes for the first time. My feet didn't have to hurt for
six months. It just went very smoothly and we progressed as a
team much like the team progressed.

Now, the first thing you have to know is Chip isn't Harry. I
think it was a little difficult for him when we left Miami and
arrived at Wrigley Field for the home opener on April 3, 1998.
It may have been one of most difficult days of his life, what
with it being the first home game after Harry's death; Dutchie
singing "Take Me Out to the Ball Game" during the seventh-
inning stretch; and the specter of Harry hanging everywhere
on the North Side of Chicago.

A lot of people were quick to criticize Chip because he
wasn't Harry, but everyone knows there can never be another
Harry, so what did people honestly expect? There were people, as well, who believed the sole reason Chip got the job was
that he was Harry's grandson and that he came out of
nowhere, but nothing could be further from the truth. Chip
did nine years of Orlando Magic basketball (1989-98), and
called baseball for the Braves (1991-92) and Mariners (1993-
95) before joining WGN at age thirty-three in 1998 with a
world of experience.

Chip was a very good broadcaster when he arrived in
Chicago and by the end of the '98 season I thought he was an

exceptional broadcaster. And here's one thing to remember: He was thirty-three when he got to Chicago and still learning, so in a few years he's going to be even better as he continues to grow into the job.

It doesn't mean anyone will forget Harry Caray, just like no one has forgotten Johnny Carson. But now it's the "Chip Caray Show" in Chicago, much like it's the "Jay Leno Show" in Burbank. Chip has shown me so much ability in one year that I think he's going to be one of those guys who can pick and choose his path as his talent takes him to the far reaches of the broadcasting business.

More importantly, he can probably be the Cubs' No. 1 man as long as he wants to be, and that's just what Harry hoped would happen when he convinced Chip to come to Chicago.

For Harry, that would have been a dream come true.

Chip is a terrific combination of both his grandfather and father. Harry was a great broadcaster. Skip continues to be an excellent broadcaster. But while Chip has taken some things from both, he hasn't tried to emulate either. He has Harry's optimism and excitement and a great deal of Skip's sardonic wit. But Chip's intelligence is far superior to that of his father or grandfather, and that's no knock on any member of Chip's family. Chip just happens to be a brilliant young man.

I appreciate him for the professional that he is and I've come to respect him as a human being. I also admire very much how dedicated he is to being a husband and father. Harry spoke about not wanting his grandchildren to make some of the same mistakes he made, and Chip obviously took those words to heart. There is nothing more important in Chip's life than his family.

The best part is when Chip's wife, Susan, brings their baby

daughter, Summerlyn, into the booth. It's almost like Harry's still with me. Summerlyn is very similar to Harry in that she tries to grab everything within her reach; she thinks everything in the booth belongs to her; she gets excited for no apparent reason; she watches everything that's happening, except what's on the field; she talks with her mouth full; and she makes inappropriate noises and screams while we're on the air.

In many ways, it's like Harry never left.

All in all, the only way it could have been a better baseball season for me was if Harry had been with us and the Cubs had won the World Series. At least once a day I would find myself thinking, "Can you imagine how much Harry would have enjoyed this season? Can you imagine how excited he would have been?" But that only made me sad, so I didn't dwell on it.

A new partner meant a new chance for me to be a color analyst again and a chance to talk a whole lot more than Harry allowed me to over the last few years. A lot of people told me I got much better at my job in my sixteenth year of Cubs baseball, but I just think I had more of an opportunity to explain things the way I was always capable of, but never really had the chance to.

That's not to say the partnership with Harry was better or worse, but the dynamic has changed. Chip and I are equal partners, while Harry and I were partners more along the lines of Ralph Cramden and Ed Norton.

This is more fun, I do have to admit that, because there's more of a challenge for me. I have to prepare a lot more because now I have the opportunity to expand on what I think and expound on what I believe.

And in the eighth and ninth innings, when Harry rarely gave me the chance to throw a word out on the air, Chip relies on me to explain what will happen before it happens and why it happened after it does.

It was a great year, 1998 was, and not just because I didn't freeze my butt off for the first time in sixteen years. (Though I was overjoyed when Chip said it was OK to put the windows in our booth in April.) There was more.

After coming off a 68-94 season in '97 and Chip replacing a legend, we could have faced that uphill climb and another moribund year of going to the ballpark every day with no hope of winning. Instead, Cubs management treated us to a fine club and one of the most exciting seasons in the history of the team.

With Sammy Sosa chasing Mark McGwire and Roger Maris for the home run record, Kerry Wood chasing the Rookie of the Year Award, and the Cubs chasing a playoff spot for only the third time since 1945, every play of every game truly meant something.

It was the first playoff race since the excitement of 1989, and I frequently thought about Harry presiding over all of those dismal years, culminating in the Disaster of '97.

"Jee-sus Chri-ist," Harry must have said. "How could you have done this to me right before this season? You could have taken me during the '94 season or the '97 season, and I wouldn't even have complained. Holy Cow! That was like a death march anyway. But you do it to me now, right before a season like this? Boy, oh boy, what a LOUSY decision."

Among so many other exciting dramas, Sammy Sosa finally blossomed into the star Harry always thought he could be. What Harry saw in Sammy was an exciting player who could light up the ballpark, much the way Ryne Sandberg did for Harry during the sixteen years they knew each other and like Stan Musial did for decades in St. Louis.

Harry loved it when a young player came up and lit up the town. He would have tried to make Kerry Wood the biggest and brightest young star in the universe. Harry realized the responsibility of the guys in the booth was to try to make stars of the players, though most of them probably don't even realize that he was hugely responsible for their popularity. Most players never understood the scope of Harry's influence, but let's face it: Harry could make or a break someone's career.

But Harry would have been in all of his glory in 1998. He would have been happy to see Mark Grace having another All-Star type season, because he adored Grace both on and off the field. He thought of him as a throwback to the old days, when guys got dirty on the field, and down and dirty off the field. He would have taken quickly to Rod Beck, what with his grizzled visage, portly appearance, gruff exterior, and high-wire acts in almost every ninth inning in which he appeared.

What a year it would have been for Harry, Chip, and me.

But knowing Harry the way I do, I have to believe he would have been tapping Chip on the shoulder every now and then, suggesting his grandson step aside for an inning or two or ten, while Harry called the Sammy Sosa at-bats and the Kerry Wood starts.

"Hey, Chip," he would have said, "why don't you take a few days off? I've given you every chance to establish yourself, but now that it's September and the Cubs are close to making the playoffs and it's all so very exciting, how about you let me finish it off?

"You're a nice young man and you've done a nice job. You got them this far, so why not let the old guy take it the rest of the way and wrap it up, huh?"

I promise you this: When it came time to call Mark McGwire's sixty-first and sixty-second homers in St. Louis, Harry would have been in the booth and Chip would have been looking for a seat in the upper deck. And when Sammy

Sosa hit four home runs in a weekend to run his total to sixty-two, Harry would have sent Chip out onto Waveland Avenue to chase after the million-dollar souvenirs. Harry loved Chip, to be sure, but Harry loved baseball more than anything else in the world.

And if the 1998 season proved nothing else, then we'll just leave it at this: Baseball loved Harry, too.

◆❖◆

After a twelve-year career in major league baseball that included a Cy Young Award and appearances in the 1979 World Series and 1980 All-Star Game, Steve Stone spent two years as a color analyst for ABC's Monday Night Baseball and the last sixteen years with WGN. He's also occasionally successful as a restaurateur, and the author of *Teach Yourself to Win*.

Barry Rozner, a sports columnist for the Arlington Heights (Il.) *Daily Herald*, has covered the Cubs and Harry Caray since the late 1980s. Rozner has won four Associated Press Awards and a Peter Lisagor Award for excellence in journalism. He has also written three books, including Ryne Sandberg's 1995 autobiography *Second to Home*.